India :

The

Social

Anthropology

Of A

Civilization

BERNARD S. COHN
The University of Chicago

INDIA :

THE

SOCIAL

ANTHROPOLOGY

OF A

CIVILIZATION

Prentice-Hall, Inc., Englewood Cliffs, New Jersey

DAVID M. SCHNEIDER, *Series Editor*

Anthropology of Modern Societies Series

Library of Congress Catalog Card Number: 76-134734

C-13-456871-O
P-13-456863-X

Current printing (last digit)

10 9 8 7 6 5 4 3 2 1

Printed in the United States of America

PRENTICE-HALL INTERNATIONAL, INC. *(London)*

PRENTICE-HALL OF AUSTRALIA, PTY. LTD. *(Sydney)*

PRENTICE-HALL OF CANADA, LTD. *(Toronto)*

PRENTICE-HALL OF INDIA PRIVATE LIMITED *(New Delhi)*

PRENTICE-HALL OF JAPAN, INC. *(Tokyo)*

To My Parents: Maybe It Was Not All for the Birds

Editorial
Foreword

The view that the proper habitat of the anthropologist is among primitive peoples has been changing. So too has the view that the anthropologist is the sociologist of backward or underdeveloped societies. More and more anthropologists have turned to modern societies for their special studies, and their work more often than not proves different in aim as well as method from the work of the sociologist working in the very same society.

It is the intention of this series to provide the student and scholar with specific examples of the application of the analytic tools and methods of an outstanding anthropologist on a particular society of the modern world. Each book focuses on a special problem or a particular way of integrating what is known about some modern society.

This particular book bridges the gap between "primitive" and "modern" societies by applying the structural-functional techniques of analysis developed in the study of the former to a society that maintained characteristics strikingly reminiscent of them *in Europe* and until the 1940's. In fact, many of the patterns described here are operative even today.

In this book India is treated as a civilization in time as well as in space, and it is shown how the present is built on the past as the future will be built on both present and past. This book is, thus, no simple-minded statement of the "ethnographic present," a kind of instant of limbo, but rather, is an account of India as a civilization through time.

There is another major point at which this book departs from the narrow confines of an older Anthropological tradition, breaking new ground in the Anthropological study of modern society. This is in its focus on process. It is not presumed that the study of one or two villages can display Indian civilization in microcosm. Neither does it single out caste, the joint family, or any other particular institutional form as the central peg on which the whole civilization is presumed to hang. It is rather the processes over time of caste, the joint family, the "Green Revolution" and so on that constitute the central methodological approach of this book.

DAVID M. SCHNEIDER

Preface

Since the end of World War II, social science has become truly international—international both in the sense that Western social scientists have discovered the world and in the sense that social science as a profession has developed enormously in the countries of the Third World. In this expansion of social science, India has bulked large. For anthropologists especially, India has been important as it has been one of the places where anthropologists have made the transition from the study of small, isolated, pre-literate populations to the study of large complex social and cultural systems which are parts of a major civilization. This shift has had major consequences for theory and method in anthropology.

In the early 1950's, it was thought that anthropologists could study an Indian village as if it were a bounded entity like a small tribe, but the first group of postwar anthropologists, Indian, American, and British, who approached villages this way, quickly realized that even at the simplest structural level, a village had to be seen in a wider context of space and time. In North India, kinship and marriage ties spread in wide networks, villages were tied into administrative and political systems which drew them into district headquarters and provincial capitals, the search for employment drew villagers into cities, mines, factories, and plantations, their religious practices drew peasants into pilgrimages and villages and into playing hosts to religious specialists who performed rituals representative of higher forms of Hinduism and Islam. Within a few years, anthropologists began to speak of the villages in which they studied not as communities, but as the loci of their research. It was found that a view of a village as a bounded system was almost impossible to maintain. Instead, the village became a site for the study of a problem, either of a theoretical nature or of some practical concern. By the late fifties, anthropologists were studying in small towns and cities, still using their methods of participant observation and interviewing. In town and urban studies, the definition of the problem of research became even more crucial because of the potentially large numbers of people involved who were not in face-to-face contact. Also, the types of social situation were numerous.

Implicit in much of the work of the anthropologist in India during the fifties and early sixties was the idea that he was sampling something. The social and cultural variation in India is enormous, both regionally and even within regions. It has been proven almost impossible to specify the universe the anthropologist was trying to sample. Were villages the unit? Were castes the unit? How many villages in a region, defined by the major language, would be sufficient to establish a scientific base for generalization? Other variables also became important. Was a small village of a single caste typical or was a large village with many castes typical? Added to these questions, the distance from a major urban center and the presence of an intensive government program directed at the improvement of agriculture had to be taken into consideration in the selection of a village for study.

In the late fifties and increasingly in the sixties, anthropologists have abandoned the simple-minded notion that one could sample. Certainly, one's research findings have to be reported with a specification of the conditions under which one worked; anthropological studies continue to be rooted in time and space, and some comparisons from one village to another and from one region to another are legitimately made. However, concern for process has replaced a concern for how representative a particular locus of research may or may not be. The study of processes such as the cultural emulation of higher groups by lower groups, the maintenance of the local hierarchy of status and power, the incorporation of Western scientific thought into indigenous thought, and the past and present effects of indigenous political systems on modern politics have become the goal. Increasingly, anthropologists have been concerned not only with analytical processes but also with the cultural models of the Indians themselves, how they perceive the situation, how they explain what is happening.

This essay is an attempt to convey what one anthropologist and historian has learned about India. It draws on the work of hundreds of other scholars. The argument of the essay is a simple one and is implicit: that a civilization, a social system, a nation exists in time as well as in space. The effort has been to see India not as it exists at a moment in time, the "ethnographic present," but how it has existed through time. In an essay of this sort, much of what I have written is conjectural, tentative, and sketchy; what I say is more exemplified than thoroughly documented.

I have been fortunate over the years in having had teachers, colleagues, and friends who have been unstinting in their generosity; they have given of their own ideas and have been patient in listening to mine. Professor Morris Opler and Dr. Rudra Datt Singh were my first guides to India. Mr. Shri Nath Singh shared much of my field and archival research. I have been fortunate to have been intermittently associated (since 1956) with the Southern Asia Committee of the University of Chicago and have benefited particularly from association with Professors Milton Singer and McKim Marriott. Professors David M. Schneider and Alfred Harris have always done their best to keep me from abandoning general concerns with social and cultural anthropology for a sole concern with things Indian. Philip Calkins, Ronald Inden, Thomas Kessinger, and Burton Stein have tried to keep me honest as an historian. Professors M. N. Srinivas, F. G. Bailey, Myron Weiner and Morris D. Morris, along with many others, will see how indebted I am to their ideas. Rella Cohn has shared the twenty-year process of learning of which this essay is one result.

The Committee on Southern Asian Studies of the University of Chicago and the Center for Advanced Studies in the Behavioral Sciences in Palo Alto provided the leisure and financial support which have made writing, if not easy, at least possible.

Chicago. July 1970

Contents

CHAPTER TWELVE

India :

The

Social

Anthropology

Of A

Civilization

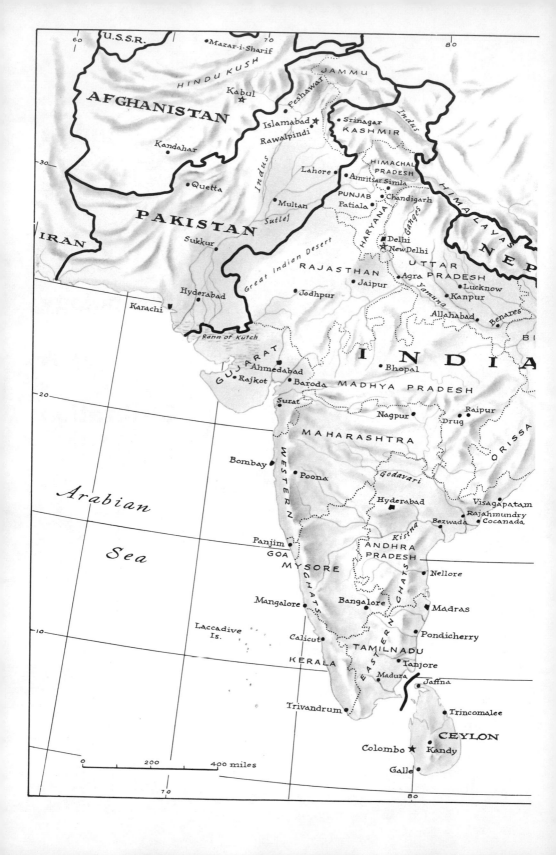

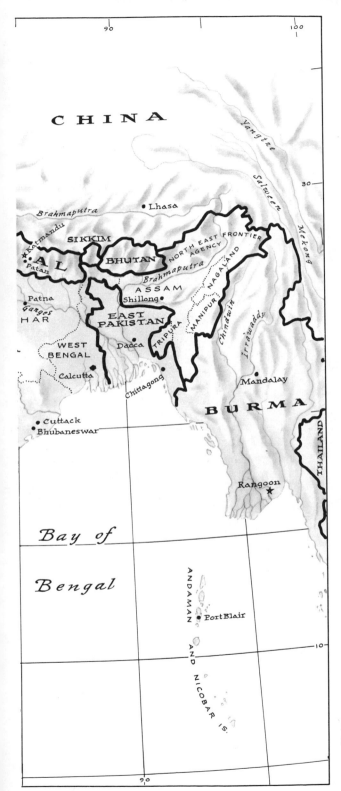

A map of India illustrating
political and topographical features.

Approaches to the Study
of Indian Civilization

It is an act of intellectual arrogance to write an essay on the social anthropology of Indian civilization. Most students of India see a continuity of tradition starting in the second millennium B.C., from the Harappan cultures that developed in the Indus Valley to the villages and cities of contemporary India and Pakistan. One can point, as W. Norman Brown has recently done, to the persistence in art of symbols, such as the pipal tree and the bull, and trace them for 3,000 years. One can trace for 2,000 years underlying, persistent, and pervasive cultural concepts, such as *dharma* (duty) or *rta* (cosmic truth or order). Other scholars have seen fundamental ideals that condition the forms of the social structure expressed in the joint family or in the caste system covering millennia. With this continuity of symbol, thought, and conception of social forms have also come great discontinuity in the political structure, major invasions both military and cultural, and wide regional variation in the way persistent and continuous traditions actually manifest themselves.

In recent years the number of specialists, both humanists and social scientists, concentrating on the study of Indian civilization has proliferated. One example of this intellectual and scholarly proliferation, a brief and sketchy catalog of the concerns of some of my present colleagues, conveys some of the diversity that must be encompassed in an understanding of Indian civilization. One colleague is developing and applying computer models to Indian cities in order to determine whether their underlying structural types differ from those of Western cities, and another is studying in a single Indian city the changing

1

form and content of cultural performances, such as dramas, rituals, and concerts in order to observe continuity and change of cultural traditions. A Sanskritist is studying philosophical texts; a political scientist is trying to understand the political behavior of opposition parties in relation to the philosophical basis of traditional Hindu political theory. One colleague is studying medieval religious texts and poetry in order to understand how a variant of Hinduism has developed, and an anthropological colleague has been studying festivals and rituals in villages in order to learn what Hinduism means to illiterate peasants. Another colleague is studying 200-year-old stories and genealogies kept by two castes in Bengal; yet another has villagers and town folk sort cards with caste names in order to see if there is consensus in the ranking of castes within local areas. A legal scholar is studying recent antidiscrimination legislation, and another has been studying the attempts of an untouchable caste in a village to raise its social status. One is studying symbolism in Tamil poetry; another, the grammar of the Munda languages spoken by a large number of tribal peoples in eastern India. A historian is studying seventeenth- and early eighteenth-century revenue arrangements introduced by Islamic conquerors; another, the effect of British administration of Indian law on indigenous social structure.

This varied activity illustrates the diversity of both the civilization being studied and the disciplines and conceptual tools used. In spite of the diversity and the methodological specialization it encourages, most of us agree that what we do is leading to a better understanding of what we call Indian. Students of India are constantly being drawn intellectually in four directions. The directions relate to underlying theories about the nature of society, culture, and civilization. One direction may be termed *cataloging*, in which the civilization is seen as consisting of specific traits that can be listed or described. Another direction is the search for a *cultural essence*, the attempt to find what has endured, not so much in terms of specific traits, but in an essential underlying process that has marked the civilization almost from its inception. A third direction concentrates on *cultural communication* and seeks to understand what is enduring about the ways the content of the civilizational system is transmitted among the parts of the society. The fourth direction sees a civilization as the local temporal working out of worldwide structural and cultural principles. This view studies India or Indian civilization as a *type*, that is, a traditional society subject to processes, such as modernization, that illustrate cultural, historical, or sociological principles.

THE CATALOG OF TRAITS

This approach postulates that there is something distinctly Indian that can be experienced, cataloged, refined, described, or measured. Variation is accounted for on the basis of statistical distribution—when we talk about India, we are talking about a statistical mean or mode. Deviations from the mode or the mean are accounted for on the basis of geographical, ecological, historical, class, or religious differences, but underlying the distribution is a trait, a quality, that is the quintessential India or partakes of Indianness.

THE DISCOVERY OF THE ESSENTIAL PROCESS

Another approach is in effect to say there is nothing quintessentially Indian in the measurable sense of particular traits or institutions. India from this view is a kaleidoscope of bits and pieces that at a particular moment is an almost haphazard, random collection of various traits, some regional, some religious, and some responding to immediate historical events. What is Indian in this view is, not content, but style and process. Indian civilization is marked by a form of absorption, of tolerance, of style of selective incorporation into a general civilizational process. W. Norman Brown, an Indologist, states this view in the following terms:

Since the third millennium B.C. India has had a highly developed civilization, and we can see that this has had a continuity through successive periods with many variations from then to the present. The variation has often been great, so that today's phenomenon looks like its antecedent, though caused by it, two or three or four thousand years ago, while there are also many differentiations in separate localities. Yet there must be something which in each successive periodic reincarnation of the civilization has caused the new existence of the civilization, something which in terms of the Buddhist doctrinal analogy corresponds to consciousness.[1]

Some have sought the essence in terms of concepts of tolerance, the acceptance of "unity in diversity"; others, in the elevation of the spiritual or the otherworldly.

[1] W. Norman Brown, "The Content of Cultural Continuity in India," *Journal of Asian Studies,* 20 (August, 1961), 429.

THE STUDY OF CULTURAL COMMUNICATION

The third approach seeks to understand the underlying system of communication and structural integration of Indian civilization. This approach sees India as a type, a civilization related to other civilizations, such as Chinese, Islamic, or medieval Western. There is less emphasis on the specific content of traditions or customs and more on how these contents are communicated through the different levels of the society. This approach takes its stimulus from the work of the anthropologist Robert Redfield. In his book *Peasant Society and Culture,* Redfield postulates that civilizations, as distinguished from primitive societies and cultures, are made up of distinct but interrelated parts or levels that have special cultural contents and styles associated with them. In its simplest form, Redfield identifies a *great tradition,* embodying the thought, values, customs, and world view of the reflective few in the society. The great tradition is associated with specialists in the maintenance and development of the tradition, the literati, the priests and ritual specialists, the cultural consumers of the cities, the royal courts, and the ritual centers. The little traditions are found among the unreflective masses, the illiterate, the uneducated, the unreflective. Economically, peasant-based societies are incomplete. Being a peasant means involvement in an economy in which agricultural products are exchanged or sold for eventual consumption by nonagriculturalists. In such an economy, the peasant needs both manufactured goods or protection offered by some governmental power above his immediate village and ritual services associated with sects or churches that are based beyond a local village cult. Culturally and socially, the system is one of interdependent parts.

There is constant cutural and social interaction between the levels with their associated traditions in Redfield's model of civilization. On examination of the content of the traditions, it seems extremely difficult to label one aspect that of the great tradition and another that of the little tradition. McKim Marriott has demonstrated that at least fifteen out of the nineteen village festivals celebrated in a small village in northern India derive from or are sanctioned by Sanskrit texts with a universal spread in India.[2] Crucial to Marriott's view of the interaction of the great and little traditions is the demonstration that the communication of rites, values, and cultural ideals has not been merely a kind of

[2] McKim Marriott, "Little Communities in an Indigenous Civilization," in McKim Marriott (Ed.), *Village India: Studies in the Little Community* (Chicago: University of Chicago Press, 1955, pp. 191–92).

elitist downward diffusion from the bearers of the great tradition but a movement upward from the little traditions as well.

For anthropologists the great tradition in India is associated with the use of the Sanskrit language for the preservation and transmission of the content of the great tradition; close analysis of what is assumed to be non-Sanskritic or of the little tradition, however, frequently turns out to be of the Sanskritic tradition. Staal, a Sanskritist, for example, argues that spirit possession, which anthropologists maintain is of the non-Sanskritic or little tradition, is actually an important part of Sanskritic traditions from their earliest known versions in the Vedas of the second millennium B.C.[3] The difficulties of sorting out the "origin" into great and little tradition, Sanskritic or non-Sanskritic, have become all too real. In addition when one tries to ask in specific terms what is the great tradition of India, one runs into the problem of the mutual coexistence of several great traditions. Is Buddhism one of India's great traditions? Historically it had its origin in India and spread to China and southeastern Asia, but today it is found in only a few border regions in northern India and in pockets in peninsular India, where it has been reintroduced in very recent time. Islam has been of significance to large numbers of the Indian population from the eleventh century to the present, but it originated outside of India. Should it be considered part of the great tradition or a separate great tradition? Since the end of the eighteenth century some Indians have begun to associate themselves with the values and forms of thought of the West. Today there are Indian atomic scientists, advertising executives, jet pilots, using mainly the English language and rejecting most outward forms thought to be typically Indian—for example, believing in the caste system, following Hindu life-cycle rites—and rejecting the idea of transmigration of souls and eternal rebirth. Is Western rationalism their great tradition?

Nonetheless, deriving from its cultural and social structure as a civilization, the process of cultural transmission can be studied and analyzed and used as a framework as one of the ways of understanding India as a civilization.

INDIA AS AN EXAMPLE OF A TYPE

The fourth approach to the study of Indian civilization is to state that, although there are distinct values, life styles, and aspects of social structure that are unique in their form and content to India, we are not

---

[3] J. F. Staal, "Sanskrit and Sanskritization," *Journal of Asian Studies*, 22 (May, 1963), 269.

interested in them. F. G. Bailey, who would call himself a comparative sociologist, puts the argument in its most extreme form:

To the Indologist what is unique in India is his interest. The comparative sociologist, on the other hand, wants to find out what India has in common with other societies—or, to phrase it more accurately, he wants to find out what, in the particular society in India he happens to be studying and which he has limited on a criterion of interaction, is found also in other societies. A definition of caste which rules out comparison with, for instance, the Southern States of America or even with South Africa, is useless for comparative sociology. The unique is scientifically incomprehensible. The unique can be comprehended only intuitively or through a mystical experience. . . . There can be no 'Indian' sociology except in a 'vague geographic sense,' any more than there are distinctively Indian principles in chemistry or biology.[4]

Bailey's position is extreme, but the point is unavoidable. Unless the scholar is to reproduce texts written by members of the society with which he is dealing or is to record only, as would someone with a movie camera fixed in one place, everything that goes on within range of his camera, he must have concepts, organizing principles, and theories of human behavior. The question that Bailey leaves unanswered is whether the concepts, organizing principles, and theories that may underlie comparative sociology, or literary criticism, in the case of students of Indian literature, are so precise, so encompassing, so powerful in explanation that they warrant the apparent ignoring of phenomena that are part of Indian civilization in its own terms. In reading the present essay, one will find the approach shifting. Some effort is made to identify the components of the civilization and show how they reveal or are shaped by underlying civilizational processes. Much attention is paid to the problem of the mechanisms of cultural and social integration, how the symbols, values, and rituals, which in their manifestation are uniquely Indian, are communicated. In order to do this, assumptions, concepts, and theories deriving from Western social science as it has developed in the last 100 years are used both to describe and to analyze India and Indian civilization. Because I have been trained as a social and cultural anthropologist, this essay can be seen as an attempt at an ethnography of a civilization. Fortes, in introducing his study of clan structure among the Tallensi of West Africa, states the problem effectively in the following terms. The writing of an anthropological monograph ". . . involves breaking up the vivid, kaleidoscopic reality of

[4] F. G. Bailey, "For a Sociology of India," *Contributions to Indian Sociology*, 3 (July, 1959), 97–99.

human action, thought, and emotion which lives in the anthropologist's notebooks and memory, and creating out of the pieces a coherent representation of society, in terms of the general principles of organization and motivation that regulate behavior in it. It is a task that cannot be done without the help of theory." [5]

Since this essay is not about a tribe of limited numbers—whose traditions are largely carried orally, in which there is little variation in custom and social structure except along a few cleavages, such as age or sex, and which is without an extensively recorded past—but about a civilization and a subcontinent of more than half a billion people, with complex, deeply rooted historical traditions, with wide variation in custom and behavior regionally and within the social structures of a particular region, it cannot be written in the field notebooks of a single anthropologist or, for that matter, the collective notebooks or monographs of all the anthropologists who have worked in southern Asia. The sources of an essay of this kind seem to be almost limitless. The particular sources I draw on, however, are essentially fourfold: first, anthropological field work in a village in northern India in the early 1950s; second, research during the last ten years on the question of the effects of the introduction of British law and administration in a region in northern India; third, in recent years, teaching modern Indian history that has forced me to broaden my view of the society in time and space to encompass much of the subcontinent; finally, during the past fifteen years, innumerable conversations in a wide series of meetings with students and colleagues concerned with all aspects of India's past and present. By now, it has become impossible for me to pinpoint the sources of many of my ideas and "facts" about India. They derive mostly from the direct experience of living in an Indian village, studying the local records of British administrators, reading what others have written, and listening and studying with fellow students who are part of a worldwide academic community.

[5] Meyer Fortes, *The Dynamics of Clanship among the Tallensi* (London: Oxford University Press, 1945), p. vii.

CHAPTER TWO

India as a Geographic Entity

The word "India'" derives from the Sanskrit word *Sindhu*, the sea, which was and is applied to the great river, now also known as the Indus, that flows through the northwestern part of undivided India. Through a sound shift common in the languages then spoken in Persia and India the initial *s* in *Sindhu* became an aspirate *h*, yielding *Hindu*, the Persian name for the river, the country near the river, and the people inhabiting the country. From the Persians in the latter part of the first millennium B.C., the name passed to the Greeks and Romans, and Hindu with some imprecision came to mean all the landmass of southern Asia—the area bounded on the northwest by the Kirhar Range, the Suliaman Range, and the Hindu Kush Mountains. These mountain ranges divided the Indus Valley from the tableland of Iran, the arid highlands of Afghanistan, and the mountains of central Asia. The Himalaya Mountains form the natural border more than 1,500 miles to the north of India, separating India from the tableland of Tibet. To the northeast a series of jungle-covered hilly tracts separates India from Burma and the mainland of southeastern Asia.

The Indians themselves did not have a definite geographic term for this land. It is clear, however, that they had a conception of the country, Bharatavarsha, "the land of the Bharatas," an ancient people mentioned in the earliest Sanskrit literature. The Indian Constitution, adopted in 1949, uses the phrase "India, that is Bharat" when talking about its name and territory. In more recent years the term "south Asia" or "southern Asia" has come to be applied to the peninsula and some adjacent states. In their recent geography text on Asia, *The Pattern of*

Asia, Norton Ginsburg and his associates include India, Pakistan, Afghanistan, Ceylon, and the mountain kingdoms of Nepal, Bhutan, and Sikkim in the geographic term "south Asia." Historically the term "India" presents difficulties because of the partition in 1947 of the Indian Empire into the two sovereign states of India and Pakistan. In this essay there is some vagueness in the use of the term "India," but, by and large, references to events or institutions before 1947 refer to undivided India and after 1947, to the present country of India, exclusive of Pakistan.

THE SOUTHERN ASIAN SUBCONTINENT IN RELATION
TO THE EURASIAN LANDMASS

The mountain barriers and the long sea coast are the two major geographic facts setting the broad cultural history of India. Looked at in general terms, the history of the Eurasian landmass from the second millennium B.C. to the fifteenth century A.D. can be seen as the rise and fall of settled agricultural civilizations based on river valleys, interacting and in conflict with the nomadic and seminomadic peoples of the steppes of central Asia. Through this period there were intermittent movements of peoples out of the central parts of the Eurasian landmass into the river valleys on the rims of the landmass. Because these movements were from west to east and east to west, not north to south, India, partially isolated, has been invaded in offshoots of the major thrust of these migrations of peoples out of central Asia.

From the movements of the Indo-Aryan-speaking peoples in the second millennium, known as the Aryans in Indian history, to the movements 1,000 years later of the Hun tribes, to the movements of the Turkic peoples from the tenth to the fifteenth century A.D., India received new populations from the northwest through the passes in the Hindu Kush Mountains. The movements and subsequent effects of these peoples once inside of India in interaction with the peoples already settled there, whether autochthons or the descendants of earlier invaders, gave Indian civilization its characteristic quality—constant inclusion of new ideas within a stable framework set during the period from 300 B.C. to A.D. 300.

Until the coming of the seaborne, nomadic Europeans in the sixteenth century, each people who came into the subcontinent broke its ties with its homeland in the landmass and became Indian. This process relates to the geography of India. Once the invaders crossed the mountains separating India from Afghanistan, it was difficult to maintain close communication over the mountains. India could not be ruled by an outside land-based power. Until 1942, when the Japanese tried to invade India from Burma on the northeast, there had never been a serious military threat to India from the northeast or over the Himalayas. In fact, there has been little contact across this frontier with Tibet and central Asia on any but a sporadic basis. It has been from the northwest, not the northeast, that India has been traditionally invaded.

From the first millennium B.C., the Arabian Sea on the west and the Bay of Bengal on the east have connected the subcontinent to a long-elaborated trade network with Persia, the lands of the Persian Gulf, the southern part of the Arabian Peninsula, the Horn and East Coast of Africa, and southeastern Asia. Although Indian sailors, traders, and craftsmen traveled in this trade network from its beginnings, trade was largely in the hands of non-Indians: Phoenicians, Persians, Greeks, Romans, Arabs, and Jews. Cultural and economic influences deriving from this early trade network tended to be isolated on the western coast of India. The Western Ghats, a range of hills that rises fairly steeply from the narrow western littoral stretching from the southern tip of India at Cape Comorin to the Satpura Range and the Narbada River 1,000 miles to the north, inhibit the large-scale movement of peoples inland from the eastern coast. Similarly, the Kathiawar Peninsula and lower parts of the Indus Valley are cut off from upper India by the Thar Desert and the broken semiarid regions of southern Rajasthan and the Malwa Plateau. The western coast of India, then, was open to outside trade and influences, but they had little long-standing effect inland.

Trade within the Bay of Bengal and to the mainland and islands of southeastern Asia was mainly in the hands of Indians. There is evidence of some connection between the eastern coast of India and southeastern Asia from prehistoric times, but only in the first millennium A.D. did this become important from a cultural-historical point of view. Its importance is seen more on the cultural landscape of southeastern Asia than on India itself. The cultures of India have been connected with the Middle East mainly by land, but also by sea, from the middle of the third millennium B.C. Trinkets and seals showing definite Indus Valley or Harappan influence have been found in Sumeria and dated at approximately 2350 B.C. Similarly, trade goods of Sumerian type have been found in the Harappan sites. The Aryans, Hellenistic Greeks, Huns, Kushans, Scythians, Persians, Arabs, and Turkic peoples all had contact and, in some cases, extraordinary impact on Indian civilization through the northwest. House types, the nature of agriculture, language, art styles, military tactics, dress, and food of northern India all show the continuing interaction of India with central and western Asia, but the basic social and political structure, religion, and world view have evidenced a consistent Indian character from the end of the first millennium B.C.

As India has been influenced since protohistorical times from the northwest, she has influenced Asia toward the southeast, particularly through the spread of Buddhism, a religion that originated in India and spread over the Himalayas to Tibet and China and through southeastern Asia. Indian civilization also had impact on the basic political and social structure of both the mainland and the islands of southeastern Asia.

The coming of the European sea-based powers changed the basic cultural-geographic structure of India. International trade, largely sea-borne, came under the control of the Europeans who, unlike their predecessors, ruled India economically and politically from newly founded coastal cities. The control of Mallaca, Aden, and the Red Sea became more crucial from the sixteenth to the nineteenth century than the passes of the Hindu Kush.

With the rise of the modern military technologies of air power and missiles, India's geographic position has changed once again. The mountain barrier of the Himalayas and the jungles of northeastern India are no longer impenetrable; and, in the seventies, with the subcontinent divided between the two major states of India and Pakistan and with China in control of the tableland of Tibet, a new political geography has emerged in southern Asia.

THE PHYSICAL GEOGRAPHY OF INDIA

Southern Asia is roughly one-half the size of the United States of America in territory but has more than three times the number of people. India is smaller than the Soviet Union, China, Brazil, Canada, or the United States. It is about 2,000 miles from the northernmost tip of Kashmir to Cape Comorin in the south. It is about 2,200 miles from Baluchistan, in Pakistan, to the eastern Assamese border of India. India lies from 8° north latitude, a point a little to the south of Panama City, to 37° north latitude, the location of Washington, D.C. The longitude of southern Asia is 68° to 98° west. India can be divided into three major physical regions.

THE MOUNTAIN ZONE

The Himalayas and the other mountain ranges of the north and northwest are, by geological reckoning, of recent age. The peaks rise sharply in the Himalayas to an average of 19,000 feet, with fifty peaks above 25,000 feet and three—Everest, Kanchanjunga, and K 2—above 28,000 feet. The valleys are V-shaped and the ridges between them rugged. In addition to contributing to the relative isolation of India and the subcontinent, the Himalayas are crucial to the soil formation, climate, and drainage of northern India. Since the Himalayas are new mountains, they are eroding rapidly, and each year, as for millennia, rich loams wash down through many streams and rivers into the plains below, where the bulk of the northern Indian population lives. Because of their height, they catch much of the precipitation coming in from the south in the form of rain and snow and feeding the many tributaries of the three great rivers of the subcontinent—the Indus, the Ganges, and the Brahmaputra. In terms of population and economy the Himalayan zone by itself is of little direct importance to India and Pakistan.

Immediately to the south of the Himalayas, stretching 1,500 miles and contributing to the traditional barrier quality of the Himalayas, is a band of jungle land, the *terai*. In the eighteenth and nineteenth centuries this was largely the abode of wild animals and a virulent malarial area. In recent years, however, the *terai,* under a vigorous program of land reclamation and clearance, is becoming an important agricultural region.

THE INDO-GANGETIC PLAIN (NORTHERN ZONE)

The flood plains of the three great rivers—the Indus, Ganges, and Brahmaputra—form an alluvial basin 2,000 miles long and 150 to 200 miles wide from the Indus Delta in West Pakistan to the delta of the Ganges and Brahmaputra in East Pakistan. The Indian part of this valley—roughly, most of the Punjab and Hiriana, Uttar Pradesh with the exception of Bundelkhand and the Himalayan districts, most of Bihar and West Bengal—contains about one-third of the Indian population on one-tenth of the land. In eastern Uttar Pradesh and western Bihar, the rural population density rises to more than 1,000 persons per square mile.

As one travels from Delhi at the western end of the plains to Calcutta, a distance of 900 miles by rail, one does not see, except fleetingly, any break on the horizon of a hill or a mountain; the plains appear completely flat. The only breaks in the monotony of the countryside are the clumps of trees, found near villages. Through much of the year the plains, with the exception of the region around Calcutta, appear dry and dusty. The northern Indian plains are literally khaki-colored, *khaki* being a Hindi word meaning dusty or dust-colored.

The Indo-Gangetic Plains can be divided analytically into four subregions mainly by the amount and distribution of rainfall, which, in turn, affect the kind of agriculture practiced in the area. These regions are the Indus Valley, the Punjab, the middle Ganges, and the lower Ganges.

The Indus Valley

Through much of its course the Indus, on its way to the Arabian Sea, travels through a very arid zone, and so agriculture is practiced mainly within a few miles of its banks. All this region is now in Pakistan.

The Punjab

This area, now divided between India and Pakistan, stretches from the hilly country west of the Indus River to 100 miles east of the banks of the Jumna River. The heart of the Punjab is the land between the five rivers—the Jhelum, the Chenab, the Ravi, the Beas, and the Sutlej—an area of about 70,000 square miles. It is difficult, as with most of the Indo-Ganges Valley, to set definite physical boundaries on subregions, such as the Punjab, but there is a break between the aridity of the Punjab proper and the relatively humid climate of the mid-Ganges area. The break comes between the Sutlej, the easternmost river of the five rivers of the Punjab, and the Jumna. Although there is variation within the region, the area around Lahore gets about 20 inches of rainfall a year, of which more than 80 percent falls between the end of June and the middle of September. Generally, major agricultural projects in India can be undertaken only in areas with 15 to 20 inches of rain and the aid of large-scale irrigation works. The southernmost part of the Punjab, Bahawalpur, gets an average of 10 inches of rain a year.

Apparently, at the time of Alexander's invasion in 326 B.C., the Punjab was a richer agricultural area than it was in the eighteenth century, but the shifting of river courses and the continuing desiccation of the region have led to the semiarid climate of the present. Since the end of the nineteenth century, however, large-scale irrigation works have again made the Punjab one of the richest agricultural regions in the Indo-Pakistan subcontinent. In 1961, on the basis of a series of criteria that included measures of both agricultural production and industrial and commercial activity, the Indian Punjab in 1961 ranked highest of all the major regions in India in terms of level of economic development as measured by the Indian census.

The Middle Ganges

The historic heartland of India-Hindustan, the Ganges or middle Ganges Valley proper, stretches from the western border (the Jumna

River, in the present state of Uttar Pradesh) to the eastern border of
Bihar, about 750 miles to the east. Its northern borders are the foothills
and swamps that lie in front of the Himalayas. Its southern borders
are the eroded margins of the uplands of central India, which range from
10 to 100 miles south of the Ganges River. In 1961, in this area of
roughly 115,000 square miles 96 million persons lived, an average
density of 836 per square mile. The overwhelming majority of this
population is rural and agricultural. Its density is exceeded only by
two much smaller subregions—the lower Ganges or Bengal, and the
lower part of the western coastal plain, Kerala—both of which are rice-
producing areas.

On the basis of rainfall the region may be divided into two sections,
following the 40-inch rain line, which runs through eastern Uttar Pradesh.
Rice can be grown on a regular basis east of this line, but it becomes
a risky crop west of it. In the early sixties, in the middle Gangetic Plain
(the eastern districts of Uttar Pradesh and Bihar) 37.5 percent of the
crop area was under rice, but in the upper Gangetic Plain only 12.4
percent. These figures compare with 76.5 percent of the crop area in
the West Bengal Plain. In the lower Gangetic Valley, 75 percent of all
land is arable and in the upper Gangetic Valley, 68 percent; of all
Indian regions, only the northern Deccan, Maharashtra, reaches this level
of intensity of cultivation. In the upper Ganges Valley, wheat, barley,
millet, and maize are the bases of the agriculture; in the lower Ganges,
these grains and rice are the important crops. Throughout the area the
principal cash crop is sugarcane, with those agriculturalists who produce
a surplus selling wheat, barley, and rice.

The Lower Ganges

The differences between the middle and lower Ganges are immediately
apparent to the eye. Much of the middle Ganges is khaki-colored during
the year, but the lower Ganges is often green and lush, abounding in
ponds, streams, rivers, and marshy areas. Most of the area gets between
50 and 60 inches of rain a year, and so the crop land is primarily under
rice—76.5 percent in 1961. The land is classified geologically as recent
deltaic, and the landforms are more unstable in the southeastern part
of the lower Ganges than in the middle Ganges.

THE MONSOON AND THE PATTERN OF CLIMATE

As is clear from the discussion thus far, rain and its distribution are
crucial to understanding the regions and agriculture of India. From the
Arabian Sea to the Sea of Japan there is an annual rhythm of winds.

Starting with the warming of the air during April, May, and June, warm, moisture-saturated air begins to move inland over the southern and eastern landmasses, hitting the coastal or inland ranges and causing the rainy season. Starting in October, the winds reverse, and there is an outflow of dry, cooler air going toward the tropical seas. This climate is called *monsoonal*, from the Arabic word for season, *mausim*.

In southern Asia the monsoonal pattern varies somewhat by region. In northern India, June to September is the heavy rainy season, with more than 85 percent of the annual rain of the middle Ganges falling during this period. Southern India has a more equal distribution of rain through much of the year, with peak precipitation in November. The west coast follows roughly the pattern of northern India, with the monsoon beginning at the end of May rather than in the middle of June.

The seasons of India are based on the relation of the rains to annual cycles of temperature. For most of India, with the exception of the south and the arid zones of the northwest, there are three major seasons. There are some differences, depending on location; for example, in the coastal regions, the rainfall is higher, the rainy season longer, and the temperature range less extreme than in the inland regions. The following description of the seasonal cycle is typical of much of inland northern India.

The Hot Season

From the middle of March to the middle of June, the daytime temperature rises gradually from the high 80s at midday in March to over 100 in May—in the shade. In the sun it can rise to 120. Added to the discomfort of the hot, dry heat for northern Indians is a daily west wind that travels over the dusty plains from midmorning to midafternoon. With the exception of the threat of cholera due to contaminated drinking water, the hot season, for all its discomforts, is a relatively healthy time of the year. At the beginning of the hot season, in late February and early March, the dry-season crops (*kharif*) of wheat, barley, peas, and gram, which were sown in November, are harvested. Starting in late March and into April, sugarcane is sown, cultivated, and irrigated. The major wedding seasons are in April and May, because there is relatively little agricultural work to be done, and with the *kharif* harvest over, there is some agricultural surplus for feasting, a major part of wedding ceremonies.

The Rainy Season

Starting early in June, clouds begin to appear in the sky as the first sign of the impending rains. In the rice-growing regions of the Ganges

Valley, workers begin to prepare the nurseries where the rice is sown initially. By mid-June the temperature begins to moderate a bit, because the cloud cover has increased. The rains may begin suddenly with deluges or gradually with a few showers. At the time of the first rains, the northern Indian farmer must gamble on the fact that the monsoon has indeed begun and that there will be heavy rains for the next two or three weeks. With the rains, begins a period of intense activity, of plowing and sowing. If the monsoon does not continue from the time when the lands have been plowed and sown with the *rabi* crops of rice, maize, and millet, the farmer is in danger of losing his investment in seed and labor.

The monsoonal rains, providing 70 to 90 percent of the rainfall of the year, are not usually steady all-day rains but come in heavy showers during part of the day or night. In a short time the countryside changes from dust to mud and from monochromatic khaki to shades of soft green, and the land begins once again to have a cover of growing plants. The rainy season is relatively unhealthy, with epidemic diseases like typhoid and cholera, and a sharp rise in fevers, particularly malaria, brought about by the swarms of mosquitos. There is intense agricultural activity until mid- or late July, when the rice seedlings are transplanted. For much of the population of northern India, directly dependent on what they can grow and store or earn as day laborers, the period from the end of July to early September, when the corn and millet begin to ripen, is one of food scarcity, because there is little labor to be done and stored food from the *kharif* crop has been used up.

The Cold Season

The rains begin to slacken in September, and fields are now prepared for the sowing of the *rabi* crops of wheat, barley, peas, and gram. The fields must be plowed and leveled. In late October and in November the fields are sown and, until January, irrigated from ponds and wells. In October and November the rice is harvested, and the cane is cut, crushed, and made into various forms of sugar and molasses. At the end of September the temperature slowly begins to moderate, with temperatures in the 80s during the day dropping into the 50s and 60s at night. By December the evenings and nights are cool, with temperatures in the 40s. To the visitor or the well-off peasant who can afford woolen clothes and blankets, the period from October to January is very pleasant. But for many of the agriculturalists who have only cotton clothing and few blankets, the nights are uncomfortable. The cold season is also a time of increase in respiratory disorders. From January, when most of the cane has been cut and the *rabi* crop has yet to ripen fully, there is another period of food shortage for the poorer agriculturalists. In February the peas and gram begin to ripen, and from the end of February, when the barley and wheat crops are harvested, is once again a time of adequate grain supplies. By the end of February the day and night temperatures begin to rise again, and by March the leaves fall off the trees, heralding the beginning of another hot season.

The annual climate cycle of rain and temperature underlies both India's agriculture, the main basis of the economy, and much of its society and culture. Traditionally, military activity was tied to the seasons, the campaign season being in October or November, when the *kharif* crop had been harvested, until the onset of the rains. By and large, the major Hindu festivals fall at the end of the two harvests. In the north, Diwali and Dashera occur at the time of the *kharif* harvest, and Holi, the "great spring festival," occurs at the close of the *rabi* harvest.

CENTRAL AND SOUTHERN INDIA

The Indo-Gangetic Plain, the semiarid regions of Rajasthan, and the coastal lands of Gujarat are separated from the southern two-fifths of India by a range of low hills lying roughly in an east-west direction. These are the Vindhya Mountains and Satpura Range in the west, the Mahedeo Hills, the Maikala and Kaimur Ranges toward the east, and the hill lands and jungles of Chota Nagpur in the east. In addition to the hills, three rivers help separate the north from the south. The Narbada, flowing east to the Arabian Sea, forms a valley between the Vindhya Mountains and the Satpura Range. The Tapti roughly parallels the Narbada to the south. The Brahmani and the Mahanadi, which flow into the Bay of Bengal, help cut off the southern peninsula on the east coast. In this upland hilly region running across the center of India lives the bulk of India's tribal peoples.

The tribal peoples of the central mountain zone occupy the slopes and spurs of the Vindhyas, Satpura, and Mahadeo-Maikal, which join the northern part of the Eastern and Western Ghats and outlying ranges, such as the Aravallis to the northwest in Rajasthan. These hills and mountains can be defined roughly by the Narbada River to the north and west and the Godavari River to the south and east. In this extensive block live almost three-quarters of the 30 million Indians recorded in the census of 1961 as belonging to the scheduled tribes.

Centering in the easternmost part of this block, the Rajmahal Hills and the Chota Nagpur Plateau, and stretching into the southeastern part of West Bengal and the northeastern corner of Orissa are three large tribes: the Santal, with 3,150,000 persons; the Oraon, with 1,440,000; and the

Munda, with 1,010,000. Also in the block are the Ho, with 450,000, and the Bhumij, with 300,000. To the south of this territory and inland, paralleling the coast in Orissa are the Khondmals, where more than 800,000 Khonds live. In the middle and western parts of this central mountain belt, the most important tribes are the Kols or Koli, 650,000 scattered along the northern fringes; the Gonds in the central part in the Satpura and Mahadeo Hills, with 3,150,000; and the Bhils, India's most numerous tribe, with almost 4,000,000 persons living in the western part of the Vindhya Mountains and Satpura Range and extending up into the Malwa Plateau and the Aravalli Hills. These nine tribes of approximately 15 million persons account for about two-thirds of the tribal peoples living in the central zone and compose approximately half of India's tribal population.

Since Independence there has been a concerted effort on the part of the national and state governments to improve the economic situation of the peoples defined as tribal. The census of 1961 used refinements of lists made in 1951 to determine who were tribals and who were not. Those defined as belonging to tribal groups are eligible for certain kinds of benefits in education and for access to government positions. In the figures given above from the census of 1961, a *tribal* is defined as someone belonging to a group whose name appears on the scheduled tribe list. The criteria used over the years to draw up these lists are a combination of location—many tribal peoples live in hilly or inaccessible areas—and linguistic and sociological customs—many speak "tribal" languages and have names or identify themselves with one of the groupings considered tribal.

The question of who is or is not a tribal has been further confused by political considerations. Since the early part of the twentieth century, with the beginning of elected representative government at the local district, state, and national levels, a system of communal or special electorates, supposed to represent and protect the interests of minority groups in the society, was developed. This system of separate or communal electorates functioned to separate Hindu and Muslim groups in society and also made the question of enumeration in the census very important. Because censuses before 1931 also recorded a person's caste and published tables listing the numbers in each caste, literate and politically oriented people became very conscious for administrative and statistical purposes of how people were labeled. Particularly in the 1930s, when tensions between Hindus and Muslims were at a peak, politicians and scholars voiced great concern over the question of who was recorded as a tribal or aborigine and what this meant. Many argued that the aborigines were only backward Hindus and that separate counting of aborigines was a device on the part of the British to make the number of Hindus in society appear smaller. Politics and political argument are reflected in the gross statistics concerning aborigines: in 1931, about 22 million were recorded as tribal or aborigine; in 1941, the number dropped to 10 million; and in 1961 it rose to 30 million. This variation reflects administrative and political considerations rather than changes in demography.

In reality, the categories of tribe and caste must be seen as a continuum reflecting ethnographic reality, since during India's long history there has been continual change of peoples from tribal social structure and culture to caste Hindus. Structurally, tribals tend to be organized along segmentary principles of groupings based on descent. When one talks of the Khonds or the Bhils, he is talking of groupings in which membership, rights, or control of resources are based on kinship (real or imagined) and which have a common language and some cultural affinities. A caste is part of a society in which groups are interdependent, hierarchically ordered, and where one or a few castes control the major resources of the society—land, for example. Tribal societies are organized according to a principle that recognizes kinship as the main tie between a person and his fellows. Traditionally, in cultural terms, the main criterion for differentiating Hindu from tribal has been to establish whether the group grants to the Brahman (the priest), rather than to its own members, primacy as a religious interpreter and instructor.

In economic terms, tribals usually have a subsistence system based on gathering forest products or slash-and-burn agriculture. Caste Hindu economy is based on plow agriculture and production for markets. Today, in the central zone, structural, cultural, and economic distinctions are far from clear. Many tribals are settled agriculturalists in their own villages, producing both forest and agricultural products for market, or they are grouped in villages with caste Hindus who interact with the tribal group as if it were a caste, with the result that it fits into the caste system, although its internal organization is different. In religious terms, it is frequently difficult to distinguish what might be tribal from what is Hindu. For centuries the tribal groups in many parts of the central zone have been in contact and have had ordered and regular relations, particularly of a political nature, with other groups in the area. Tribes such as the Bhils were for a long time incorporated into the political and military system of the Rajputs of Rajasthan and Gujarat as auxiliaries and mercenaries.[1]

[1] Figures for the various tribal groups and other statistical materials are to be found in the Provincial volumes of the 1961 census, devoted to schedule tribes and castes. For discussion of analytical problems involved in the concept of tribe, see

THE SOUTHERN PLATEAU

South of the central mountain zone lie the southern plateau, the southern uplands, the two coastal plains, and the important deltas, which are the main southern agricultural regions. As in the north, the river system gives the south its distinctive geography. The important river systems of the south are the Godavari, the Kistna, the Penner, and the Cauvery, all of which rise in the Western Ghats, a range of hills paralleling the western coast, the Konkan and Malabar Coastal Plains. All these river systems start within 50 miles of the Arabian Sea and flow east until they empty into the Bay of Bengal. The rivers, for much of their distance, travel through hills and sharp gorges and have rapids and falls, unlike the northern river systems, which flow through broad and gradual plains to the seas. The southern rivers are not navigable for much of their course and are difficult to cross, particularly in the rainy seasons. Following John Brush, the geographer, southern India can be divided into seven regions: the Dekkan Plateau (most of the state of Maharashtra); Gujarat and Kathiawar (the state of Gujarat); the Konkan Coast (the coastal parts of Maharashtra and Goa); the Malabar Coast (the state of Kerala); the Southern Dekkan (Mysore and the upland parts of Andhra Pradesh); the Madras Coast (the present state of Madras); the Andhra-Orissa Coast (the coastal parts of Orissa and Andhra Pradesh).

F. G. Bailey, " 'Tribe' and 'Caste' in India," *Contributions to Indian Sociology,* 5 (October, 1961), 7–19; for the distribution of the tribes and discussion of general characteristics of tribal groups, see B. S. Guha, "The Indian Aborigines and Their Administration," *Journal of the Asiatic Society, Letters and Science,* 17 (Bengal, 1951), 19–44. The monographic literature on India's tribal peoples is very large and of varying quality. Three recent and theoretically significant works on tribal peoples are F. G. Bailey, *Tribe, Caste and Nation* (Manchester, England: University of Manchester Press, 1960), which emphasizes the political interrelations of tribals with villagers; Martin Orans, *The Santal* (Detroit: Wayne State University Press, 1965), which discusses what happens to a tribal people in a modern industrial setting; and Robbins Burling, *Rengsanggri: Family and Kinship in a Garo Village* (Philadelphia: University of Pennsylvania Press, 1963), which is directed to problems of kinship. Surajit Sinha, in a series of important articles, has explored the relations of tribal to Hindu in eastern and central India in terms of the nature of cultural and social change. See particularly "The Media and Nature of Hindu-Bhumij Interactions," *Journal of the Asiatic Society, Letters and Science,* 23 (Bengal, 1957), 23–37; "Tribal Cultures of Peninsular India as a Dimension of Little Tradition in the Study of Indian Civilization: A Preliminary Statement," *Journal of American Folklore,* 71 (1958), 281, 504–18; "State Formation and Rajput Myth in Tribal Central India," *Man in India,* 42 (1962), 35–80; and "Tribe-Caste and Tribe Peasant Continua in Central India," *Man in India,* 45, 1, 1965, 57–83.

The Dekkan Plateau

The Dekkan Plateau region is marked by a very rich black soil caused by the weathering of the widespread lava flow that is its underlying geological structure. The area is intensively cultivated, but yields are relatively low because of the difficulties in irrigating. Millets, maize, and pulses account for more than 60 percent of the crops grown. Cotton is the main cash crop. The Dekkan Plateau is the homeland of the Marathi-speaking peoples.

Gujarat and Kathiawar

This region is not so easily defined by geographic features by itself as it is by differences from the four regions that bound it: the Sind in Pakistan to the north, an arid, flat zone; Rajasthan to the northeast; the uplands of the central hill zone of Madhya Pradesh to the east; and the Dekkan Plateau to the south. There are three distinct physical parts to Gujarat and Kathiawar. The first is the area around the Rann of Cutch, containing mud flats to the south, and desert to the north, toward the Pakistan border. Little agriculture is practiced here. The second, the Kathiawar Peninsula, is generally semiarid, with rainfall varying from 15 to 20 inches along the northern coast to 40 inches inland to the south. Kathiawar receives considerable irrigation from ponds and wells and produces wheat and cotton.

The third, Gujarat proper, lies east of Kathiawar and to the south along the coast. Much of the area consists of alluvium soils formed by the Sabarmati and Mahi Rivers. Rainfall is heavy along the coast, ranging from 60 to 70 inches, but this drops to 30 to 40 inches inland. Cotton and millet are the main crops.

The Konkan Coast

The Konkan Coast stretches 30 to 50 miles wide, from north of the city of Bombay 450 miles down the coast. It is separated from the Dekkan Plateau by the Western Ghats, a range of hills that, although only 2,000 to 3,000 feet high, rises very abruptly from the coastal plain. The Ghats to some extent cut off the littoral from the uplands and provide the coastal plain with a high rainfall, because the monsoons drop much of their rain when they hit the Ghats. The slopes of the Ghats are heavily wooded, and about 30 percent of the land of the region is under forest cover. Rice, the main crop produced along the coast, covers about half of the agricultural land.

The Malabar Coast

Malabar stretches along the southwestern coast 450 miles from south of the 14° north latitude to the southernmost tip of Cape Comorin. It ranges about 30 to 40 miles inland and is cut off from Madras by the Western Ghats, which are higher and more precipitous than along the Konkan Coast to the north, with average heights of 5,000 feet rising to over 8,000 feet in the Nilgiris. Malabar, a rich agricultural region, is very intensively cultivated, mainly in rice. Only 46 percent of the area of the region is arable, but on this land the average population density is 1,700 to the square mile, by far the highest ratio of man to cultivated land in any region of India. The rain is heavy and reliable, with 80 to 200 inches along the coast. Rice is the main crop, with coconuts, tea, coffee, and pepper the important cash crops in the hills.

The Southern Dekkan

Inland from the southern Konkan Coast and Malabar is a hilly plateau, about 1,000 to 3,000 feet above sea level. It is cut by many rivers and streams and occasional peaks. It is semiarid, with 30 to 40 inches of rain, and is less rich agriculturally than the Dekkan to the north, with its black soils that retain the moisture better. The population is relatively scattered and depends on the growing of millet, maize, and pulse as its staple crops.

The Madras Coast

There are two subregions—the broad coastal plains and the river deltas, which are very rich rice-growing lands, well watered by ponds and irrigation facilities as well as rain. Inland from the coast there begins a series of hills and uplands that do not have the rugged quality of the Ghats farther to the north. These hills do rise quite steeply, however, on the border between western Tamilnad and the Malabar Coastal Plain. This is a millet area and tends to be somewhat drier. In the hills, coffee and tea are important commercial products.

The Andhra-Orissa Coast

To the north of Madras along a coastal plain 50 to 60 miles wide, 700 miles long, and stretching up to Bengal, are the Andhra-Orissan Coastal Plains, a very rich agricultural zone heavily dependent on rice. The rise of the Eastern Ghats is fairly sharp in Andhra and into Orissa. The region

has never had political or cultural unity but is rather a series of deltas—
to the north, the Mahanadi and Brahmani systems and, to the south in
Andhra, the Godavari and Krishna Deltas. The rivers were traditionally
difficult to cross until the building of railroads. The rainfall increases
as one goes north, and so rice becomes the most important crop.[2]

[2] The briefest and most useful introduction to the geography of southern Asia is
found in the chapters by John Brush (pp. 458–677) in Norton Ginsberg (ed.), *The
Pattern of Asia*, Englewood Cliffs, N.J.: Prentice-Hall, 1958. A new edition of this
valuable book is to appear shortly. The standard work is O. H. K. Spate, *India and
Pakistan: A General and Regional Geography*, 3rd ed., London: Methuen, 1967.
Much of the economic data in the work unfortunately is out of date.

CHAPTER THREE

Cultural and Historical Geography

As F. J. Richards, the archaeologist, has shown, the basic physiography of the southern Asian subcontinent—the river and mountain systems—has set a loose framework for a persistent political, cultural, and historical pattern. The historical geography of India can be seen as the persistent interaction, until very recent years, of three kinds of zones: *perennial* or *nuclear zones, route zones,* and *zones of relative isolation.*[1]

NUCLEAR ZONES

The nuclear zones are the river basins and plains. Starting with northwestern India, the first major nuclear zone is Gandhara, the area to the north of the Salt Ranges around Peshawar, the present capital of Pakistan. This is the area where invaders from the northwest—the Aryans, Greeks, and successive waves of Islamic peoples—first established them-

[1] Most discussions of the cultural geography of India begin with F. J. Richards's seminal article, "The Geographical Factors in Indian Archaeology," *The Indian Antiquary,* vol. 62, 1933, pp. 235–43. Other useful discussions about historical geography are W. M. Day, "Relative Permanence of Former Boundaries in India," *Scottish Geographical Magazine,* vol. 55, 1949, pp. 113–42; A. II. K. Spate, *India and Pakistan: A General and Regional Geography,* London, 1954, pp. 144–70; K. M. Pannikar, *Geographical Factors in Indian History,* Bombay, 1955; and B. Subbarao, *The Personality of India,* Baroda, 1958, pp. 8–35. There are two excellent recent studies by anthropologists, discussing, in terms of major regions, the relationship among history, society, culture, and ecology: Joan P. Mencher, "Kerala and Madras: A Comparative Study of Ecology and Social Structure," *Ethology,* vol. 5, no. 2, April, 1966, pp. 135–71; and Gerald Berreman, "Peoples and Culture of the Himalayas," *Asian Survey,* vol. 3, no. 6, June, 1963, pp. 289–304.

selves. It has been a region characterized by its role in transmitting influences from western and central Asia into India.

The Punjab, the land of the five rivers between the Jhelum and the Sutlej, is a difficult area to characterize culturally, tending to be transitional between the center around Peshawar or over the Hindu Kush into Afghanistan and cultural-political centers around Delhi and Agra.

The Sutlej-Jumna Doab and the Ganges Jumna Doab—Kurushetra and Panchala—are also major nuclear zones. *Doab* is the Hindi word for the land between two rivers. In this area, referred to in Sanskrit literature as the Madhyadesha, or middle land, classical Hindu culture took its form in the period from the fifth century B.C. to the third century A.D. Its northern boundary is the Terai and the Himalayas; its western boundary the Thar Desert and the Aravali Range; and its southern boundary the Vindhya Mountains. Politically these two *doabs* tended to be divided, with one center in the east at Kanauj or Ajodhya and another in the west in the area around Delhi and Agra. Geographically the western part, known as Kurushetra, is the plains to the west of Delhi, the battleground of the epic Sanskrit poem *The Mahabahrata*. The area to the east is Kosala or Panchala.

Kurushetra is the traditional battleground of northern India, because the area around Delhi is the last geographic barrier to a military or folk conquest from the northwest of India. The Aravali Range juts up from the southwest toward the Himalayas, and the Jumna is the last major river line before the rich Ganges plains. In the plains northwest of Delhi, usually at or near Panipat, various armies fought again and again for control of northern India. With control of the Delhi region, an army could turn eastward toward the middle and lower Ganges, where there were no natural barriers until the eastern border of Bihar, where the Rajmahal Hills, the northeastern extremity of the central mountains that divide India almost from the Arabian Sea to the Bay of Bengal, reach nearly to the Ganges River. Also, from Delhi an army could turn southwest through Malwa toward Gujarat or the Deccan.

The borders of the cultural zones from the Sutlej to the Bay of Bengal are not sharply defined. The western end of the area from the northern end of the Jumna Ganges Doab to the Sutlej is clearly different historically and culturally from the southeastern end in Bengal, but whether the land between should be one or two distinct zones—one centering on Kosala or Oudh and another centering on Bihar north of the Ganges River, Mithila—is an open question.

Bengal, in terms of the relative lateness of its colonization compared with the rest of the Ganges Valley, its differences in religion—Buddhism persisted longer than in other parts of India and there was extensive

Muslim conversion particularly in the east—its dependence on rice agriculture, and its deltaic physiography, which leads to a different settlement pattern from most of the Ganges Valley, is clearly a distinct cultural zone. Assam to the northwest of Bengal, the valley of the Brahmaputra, and the area down the Bay of Bengal to the area around the mouths of the Mahnadi River, the country of the Kalingas, and present-day coastal Orissa are strongly influenced by Bengali culture.

The cultural zones of the Ganges Valley, then, can be seen as Kurukshetra or the Sutlej-Jumna Doab with influence into the Ganges-Jumna Doab; Kosala or present-day central Uttar Pradesh with influences into eastern Uttar Pradesh and with a vague gradual border to northern Bihar or Mithila; and Bengal with outlying influence into Assam and the Kalinga or Orissa Coast as a transition zone or route zone between southern India and Bengal. The lower basin of the Indus or the Sind is a distinct cultural zone and was one of the first areas successfully Islamicized. The other nuclear zone in the north is Saurahstra or Gujarat.

ZONES OF RELATIVE ISOLATION AND ROUTE ZONES

The Ganges Valley and the plains of the Indus, cut off from the bulk of the subcontinent by the Thar Desert, are a region of relative isolation. This area, known as Rajputana or Marwar, has been populated from the tenth century on by Rajputs and other refugee peoples pushed by Islamic invaders. The Rajputs, descending from the last Hindu rulers of the north and defeated by Islamic peoples in the period 1000 to 1200, elaborated a military-political system in the semiarid zones of Marwar. They established their culture over scattered tribal peoples, particularly in the Aravali Range.

South of the Aravali Range is the Malwa Plateau, a semiarid but not impassable tableland. Malwa is a classic case of the third kind of cultural region found in India, the shatter or route zone, connecting northern India with the western coast and the Deccan. The shatter or route zone consists of the regions through which large numbers of people have passed in either military or peaceful invasion. These areas, in effect, connect the nuclear regions of attraction and have no persistent political tradition or tradition of unity of their own, as the nuclear zones and the zones of relative isolation tend to have. Socially and culturally, shatter or route zones are mosaics rather than highly distinctive cultures with diagnostic aspects of social structure. Of the twenty-three principal castes in Malwa, no less than fifteen have traditions of migration from outside and connections with various invading peoples who pass through the zone.

In the northern half of India there are several other zones of relative isolation, all of which are hilly or mountainous. The first of these lies within the Northern Mountain Arc. All across the northern frontier of the subcontinent from the Kirthan Range near the Arabian Sea, which separates Sind, the Indus Valley, from the southern part of the tableland of Iran, through the Suliman Range and Hindu Kush Mountains, which separate West Pakistan from Afghanistan, is a series of loosely organized tribes, who lead a semimilitary, semipastoral way of life in the hills and mountains and practice settled agriculture in the valleys. Since the end of the first millennium they have been Islamicized and little subject to consistent political control. To the south, on the Iranian border, these tribes are called Baluchis, and to the northwest, on the Afghan border, Pathans. Farther to the north are the Dards. The tribes tend to be localized in relatively self-sufficient communities, only loosely tied to other such groups and composed internally of communities or tribal segments differentiated by kinship and occupation into functional groups called *quom*. The difficulty of the terrain and their location in a shatter zone between several major political structures of the "tribes" have for centuries made these groups very difficult to control.

The area around Gilgit and Jammu and Kashmir is another zone of isolation in the Kashmir Valley, having a distinctive culture based on settled agriculture and assimilating refugee peoples from the plains. To the southwest of Jammu and Kashmir but in the highlands, as the Himalayas swing down toward the plains, all along the northern border through the independent state of Nepal and the semi-independent states of Bhutan and Sikkim, to a place where the Brahmaputra River enters the plains of Assam, one finds a double cultural and social structure: a basic Tibetan culture, with forms of Buddhism as the religion of the bulk of the population engaged in pastoralism or agriculture in the valleys and cross-Himalayan trade, with strong Hindu influences brought by refugee plains peoples who often were able to establish themselves as rulers of the Tibetan peoples. The Hindu-plains influence is strongest in the hill states of the Punjab, the present Himacahal Pradesh, and through the hills along the Uttar Pradesh, Tibet, and Nepal borders, but the culture becomes much more Tibetan in the eastern third of the Himalayas. To the northeast of India is a series of jungle-clad hills and mountains on the border between Burma and India. This is another zone of isolation, including the population of highland Assam and the Northeast Frontier Agency. There is a relatively sharper distinction between hill peoples, who are termed tribal, and the plains Assamese than appears in the western end of the Himalayas. The major groups here are the Nagas, the Khasis, and the Garos. Most of these tribes speak a Mon

Khmer language, although the Khasis speak Tibeto-Burman. The hill peoples uniformly look mongoloid, and their culture is the westernmost extension of a general type found in highland southeastern Asia. Most are slash-and-burn agriculturalists, growing dry rice and other grains. They are relatively unstratified and have held a fascination for the anthropologist because of the presence of matrilateral cross-cousin marriage.

There are two other major zones of relative isolation in northern central India, both of which are associated with hilly and relatively inaccessible country. The Vindhya Mountains, 1,500 to 3,000 feet high, run from the eastern part of Gujarat, north of the Narabada River, almost to the Ganges east of Banaras, where from the river the terminal hills of the Kaimur Range can be seen. To the south of the Narabada River and the Vindhya Mountains is another series of mountains and hills through northern Maharashtra, Madhya Pradesh, northwestern highland Orissa, and southeastern Bihar in the Chota Nagpur Plateau. The culture and social structure of the tribal peoples were discussed in Chapter 2.

The central zone of relative isolation, with its broken terrain and tribal population, is a transition zone, dividing India into two major cultural zones: the Indo-Aryan-speaking north and the Dravidian-speaking south, with the exception of southern Maharashtra. The transitional quality of this central belt is reflected in the fact that some of the tribes speak Mundari languages, a distinct language family separate not only from the Tibeto-Burman of the Himalayan fringe and the northeastern tribal area but also from the Indo-Aryan of the north and the Dravidian of the south. Other tribes, such as the Bhils, speak an Indo-Aryan language, and still others speak Dravidian languages.

THE NUCLEAR ZONES OF THE SOUTH

The five major nuclear zones of southern India are Andhra, Tamilnad, Kerala, Maharashtra, and Mysore. Andhra, the Telugu-speaking country based on the rich agricultural deltas of the Godavari and Kistna Rivers and the coastal plain, extends northward toward Orissa and inland into the central southern plateau. In cultural terms, though, the coastal lowlands were the nuclear area. To the south of Andhra along the eastern coast, based on the plains Pennar River and Cauvery delta farther to the south, is Tamilnad, composed of the present state of Madras on the coastal plain and the hills of the Eastern Ghats down to the tip of India at Cape Comorin. Historically this was the site of the Chola and Pandyan kingdoms. The southwestern littoral of Kerala or Malabar, the homeland of the Malayalam speakers, is relatively isolated from the rest of southern India by the Western Ghats, which are precipitous and relatively high, rising to 8,000 feet in the Nilighiris. As one approaches Kerala from the Arabian Sea, they appear to rise quite sharply. There is only one main and easy pass through the southern part of the Western Ghats, the Palghat or Coimbatore Gap, which gives access to Tamilnad. A distinctive culture and social structure were elaborated in this narrow coastal plain: matrilineal succession for major groups; the presence of a military caste, the Nayars; the most stringent regulation controlling the behavior of the Untouchables in any region of India; and a dispersed settlement pattern of the villages. The other two nuclear zones of southern India are Maharashtra, the Maharati-speaking area of the Dekkan Plateau, and Mysore, the Kanerese-speaking part of the inland plateau down to the coastal area north of Kerala. Unlike the other nuclear zones of the south, the two inland ones are not based on rice and river deltas and coastal littorals, as are Andhra, Tamilnad, and Kerala, but on dry agriculture, particularly millet and more recently maize and gram. There is a fairly dispersed settlement pattern compared with the nucleated villages of the upper Ganges Valley and the villages of the Tamilnad. The northern part of Maharashtra, the Khandesh, is a transition zone from the north. Marathi-speaking areas did not achieve a cultural unity until the seventeenth century, when, under Shivaji, there developed a short-lived political entity. In the eighteenth century the Marathas, based on the northern Dekkan highlands around Poona, developed a large-scale empire that covered much of northern and central India. Through the highlands, just back from the western coast, there is a hilly region associated with the Western Ghats, an area of relative isolation. In these hills still live the remnants of tribal populations or groups, such as the Coorg, who live in the Western Ghats between the old states of Mysore and Malabar. This tribal zone of relative isolation stretches down most of the Western Ghats. In the central Eastern Ghats, in what is today southern Andhra and northern Madras, there is another zone of relative isolation.

SUMMARY OF CULTURAL GEOGRAPHY

The nuclear zones of attraction developed in the river valleys or the uplands of some of the major river valleys. Here, settled agriculture based on wet rice and grain and millet could support fairly large-scale populations; there were trade centers in agricultural products as well as craft products, such as cloth and luxury goods in metal. The major premodern cities were found in these areas. Most of the nuclear zones had persistent political centers and relatively stable state systems. These nuclear zones tended, with the exception of the Ganges Valley, to be separated by zones of relative isolation associated with the highlands and tending to be populated by groups classified as tribals or by refugee peoples from the nuclear zones. The main zones of isolation were the mountain arc to the north, a central zone associated with the Vindhya Mountains cutting the subcontinent across the middle, a northeastern zone, a zone down the west coast, and one down the east coast. There were persistent patterns of relations between the perennial nuclear zones and the zones of relative isolation, with the people of the plains who had settled in agricultural areas pressing up into the hills to exercise political and military control over the hill peoples, with varying degrees of success. From time to time, a political military power based in one of the nuclear zones expanded into other regions of attraction. The lines of advance in historical times have tended to follow the same pattern, which is governed by the geography of the subcontinent.

The Mughals of the sixteenth and seventeenth centuries, the Marathas of the early and mid-eighteenth century, and the British from the middle of the eighteenth to the middle of the nineteenth centuries each had a different primary base of expansion in the subcontinent. The Mughals established themselves in the middle of the sixteenth century in the area around Delhi and Agra and then turned eastward down the Ganges Valley and penetrated to the Bengal Delta and down the Orissa Coastal Plain. Almost simultaneously they moved toward the Gujarat coast through Marwar or Rajasthan. Then, somewhat later, they moved through Malwa to the Deccan Plateau and mounted their conquest of southern India in the seventeenth century from the Western Ghats eastward across Mysore to Tamilnad. The Marathas based in the Deccan highlands moved, under Shivaji, first across Mysore to establish themselves in Tamilnad in Tanjore; then, in the eighteenth century, they reversed the direction that the Mughals had followed, moving through Malwa and Mewar to the Delhi Agra area and from there eastward down the Ganges Valley. They were one of the few political powers that thrust across central India directly to Orissa and Bengal.

The British, moving from three bases on the coast—Madras, Calcutta, and Bombay—followed the traditional routes of conquest but in different directions: from Calcutta, by stages up the Ganges Valley to the Delhi Agra region, and then into the Punjab and to the Hindu Kush in the opposite direction of the traditional pattern—from over the mountains across the Punjab and down the Ganges Valley. From Madras they moved inland, across the southern part of the peninsula against the

Kanerese and Marathi areas, and, from Bombay, into Gujarat and up to the Indus Valley to the outlying regions of the Persian tablelands. Although the directions and bases in each instance are different, the thrust lines of political-cultural advance have been mainly the same since the sixteenth century.

CHAPTER FOUR

Demography, Economic Structures, and Language

DEMOGRAPHY

In 1961, the date of the last decennial census in India, the Indian population was approximately 439,200,000 persons. The total population of southern Asia was approximately 554,000,000 (see Tables 1 and 2).

The size itself of the Indian population is an important sociological fact; the population is almost 2½ times that of the United States living on less than half of the land area. More important than size, however, are several other facts. The population per square mile in India is 358. Of this, the overwhelming bulk, 360 million, or 82 percent, is classified as rural, and a little less than 80 million, or 18 percent, as urban. The most significant aggregate figure about the population in relation to resources is ratio of rural population to cultivated square mile, which is approximately 650.

TABLE 1

Area and population of the countries of southern Asia, 1961

Country	Area, Square Miles	Population
India	1,232,000	439,235,000
Pakistan	392,000	93,832,000
Ceylon	25,000	10,625,000
Nepal	54,000	9,388,00
Bhutan	18,000	750,000
Sikkim	3,000	163,000
Total	1,724,000	553,993,000

TABLE 2

Area and population of selected countries

Country	Area, Square Miles	Population
China	3,769,000	646,530,000 (approx. 1957)
India	1,232,000	439,200,000 (1961)
U.S.S.R.	8,708,000	218,000,000 (est. 1961)
U.S.	3,549,000	179,323,000 (1960)
Indonesia	735,000	96,385,000 (1961)
Pakistan	392,000	93,832,000 (1961)
Japan	148,000	93,419,000 (1961)

The pattern of population growth (see Table 3) is also important. The population of India, although increasing since 1921, began to accelerate greatly in absolute terms as well as percentages in 1941. Although India is still overwhelmingly rural, the urban sector has been increasing at a much more rapid rate, particularly since 1941, in every state except Uttar Pradesh. In every state the urban population has at least doubled since 1941. The overall growth of the Indian population has been 1.7 percent per year since 1941 with 2.2 percent of the growth since 1951. This increase is attributable to both the decline in the death-rate and the increase in the birthrate. Life expectancy in India has risen from 23 years in 1901 to 42 years in 1961.

The significance of the distribution and the rate of growth of the population is obvious in terms of pressure on the economic basis of the society. Although experts argue greatly about the exact magnitude of the problem of the continuing population pressure on resources, they all agree that the standard of living of the Indian people, although it has in the aggregate risen somewhat since 1941, has not risen too greatly. In a society in which a large proportion of the population is at a bare subsistence level, the continued growth of the population in relation to a relatively slow expansion of agricultural and industrial production is a major problem.

Economic Structure

In 1961, 189 million persons, or 43 percent of the Indian population, were recorded by the Indian census as being gainfully employed. The overwhelming bulk of these, more than 137 million, were directly engaged in agriculture and food production (see Table 4).

The key resource in a rural economy, of course, is land. The question of land ownership in India is complicated. Before the early fifties, when

TABLE 3

Population growth, 1901–1961

	1961			1941			1921			1901		
	Total	Rural	Urban	Total	Rural	Urban	Total	Rural	Urban	Total	Rural	Urban
India	439	360.3 (170)*	78.9 (305)*	319	(129)*	(171)*	251	(105)*	(109)*	236	(100)*	(100)*
Andhra P.	36.0	(172)	(341)	27.3	(137)	(199)	21.4	(112)	(137)	19.1	(100)	(100)
Assam	11.9	(302)	(1093)	7.4	(197)	(284)	5.2	(138)	(166)	3.7	(100)	(100)
Bihar	46.5	(162)	(357)	35.2	(127)	(173)	28.1	(103)	(106)	27.3	(100)	(100)
Gujarat	20.6	(217)	(262)	13.7	(148)	(161)	10.2	(115)	(101)	9.1	(100)	(100)
Jammu and Kashmir	3.6	(150)	(374)	2.9	(129)	(244)	2.4	(109)	(169)	—	(100)	(100)
Kerala	16.9	(242)	(562)	11.0	(166)	(263)	7.8	(120)	(150)	6.4	(100)	(100)
Madhya P.	32.4	(180)	(317)	24.0	(140)	(161)	19.2	(99)	(115)	16.9	(100)	(100)
Madras	33.7	(149)	(330)	26.3	(128)	(190)	21.6	(110)	(126)	19.3	(100)	(100)
Maharashtra	39.6	(176)	(347)	26.8	(131)	(176)	20.5	(105)	(120)	19.4	(100)	(100)
Mysore	23.6	(160)	(321)	16.3	(118)	(168)	13.4	(101)	(112)	13.1	(100)	(100)
Orissa	17.5	(164)	(436)	13.8	(133)	(162)	11.2	(108)	(111)	10.3	(100)	(100)
Punjab	20.3	(139)	(262)	16.1	(117)	(155)	12.5	(90)	(95)	13.3	(100)	(100)
Rajasthan	20.2	(193)	(212)	13.9	(134)	(137)	10.3	(101)	(95)	10.3	(100)	(100)
Uttar Pradesh	73.7	(176)	(149)	56.5	(115)	(130)	46.7	(97)	(92)	48.6	(100)	(100)
West Bengal	34.9	(177)	(4.3)	23.2	(124)	(229)	17.5	(101)	(122)	16.9	(100)	(100)

* Index.

SOURCE: Census of India, Part A i, p. 54, and Census of India, paper 1 of 1962, pp. 8–9.

TABLE 4

Occupational structure of India, 1961 (in millions)

1. Agriculture and food production		137.2	72.6%
a. Cultivators	96.6		
b. Laborers	31.5		
c. Plantation workers	1.2		
d. Others, e.g., livestock, fishing	4.9		
Total	137.2		
2. Manufacturing		17.6	9.3%
a. Textiles		6.5	
Nonhousehold	2.9		
b. Wood, wood products		2.2	
Nonhousehold	0.6		
c. Leather products		0.8	
Nonhousehold	0.3		
d. Chemicals *		0.3	
e. Earthware products		0.7	
Nonhousehold	0.2		
f. Basic metals production			
and manufacture		1.2	
Nonhousehold	0.8		
g. Machinery		0.8	
h. Other		1.7	
Total		17.6	
3. Services		16.3	8.6%
a. Public service, e.g., police	3.4		
b. Education	1.8		
c. Medical	.6		
d. Religious	.4		
e. Legal	.1		
f. Business service, e.g.,			
accounting	.1		
g. Community service	.1		
h. Recreation	.2		
i. Personal service e.g., laundry,			
domestics	4.2		
j. Other	5.4		
4. Trade and commerce	7.6		4.0%
5. Transportation storage, communications	3.0		1.6
Railways	1.0		
6. Construction	2.0		1.1
7. Mining and quarrying	0.9		0.5
8. Other	4.4		2.3
			100.0%

* Where there is no breakdown by household and nonhousehold, all or almost all production is nonhousehold.

all the Indian states passed land-reform acts designed to eliminate large landholders and intermediaries between the cultivators and the state, there were several kinds of landholders and many, many kinds of tenants. Before the abolition of large-scale landlords, it was useful to think of three kinds of persons with a direct interest in cultivation: owners of land, permanent tenants, and nonpermanent tenants. There was great variation from state to state in the amount of land owned by landlords, the rights they had, and the amount of income they enjoyed from their landholdings. By and large, however, in each state a very small percentage of the landholding population owned the bulk of the land. For example, in the largest state, Uttar Pradesh, in 1947 there were more than 2 million persons having the legal status of landlords. The bulk of these (85 percent), however, were small holders and paid less than 25 rupees per year as land revenue. Three thousand landlords, or about 1.5 percent, of the total number owned three-fifths of the land, and 390 landlords out of the 2 million paid 23 percent of the total land revenue in the state.[1]

As important as the concentration of landholding before the days of land reform was, its social and economic consequences are sometimes misunderstood. The situation was not one of a single landlord and great hordes of tenants at a bare subsistence level under the big landlord. In fact, in the rural social and economic structure, the most important person was not and is not the large landholder, but the small landholder and the substantial permanent tenant. More significant than the question of legal definitions of land ownership and the percentages of the land held by very big landlords is the question of who controls cultivation and allots the acreage that families cultivate. This was as true before landlord abolition as it is now. Cultivation, in Indian census or economic survey terms, is a hard category to define.

Obviously, in order to produce an agricultural product, someone must plow, sow, weed, irrigate, cultivate, and reap the crop. In some instances, those who are classified as cultivators do all this work themselves or with the help of the members of their household. In other instances, cultivators hire labor by the day, week, or season to do the farm work, although legally they are still classified as cultivators. In still other instances, cultivators are those who rent out land on a sharecropping or cash basis. Since the early fifties, in all but a very small percentage of cases, the term "cultivator" has come to refer to a person economically or legally defined as such, who directly supervises or engages in agricultural production. In Uttar Pradesh at least (see Table 5), the legal aboli-

[1] Baljit Singh and Shridhar Misra, A Study of Land Reforms in Uttar Pradesh (Honolulu, 1965), p. 27.

TABLE 5

*Cultivation of land in Uttar Pradesh. Sample villages before and
after landlord abolition*

Kind of holding, acres	Before, percent		After, percent	
	Cultivator	Cultivated	Cultivator	Cultivated
Small, 5 and below	52	17	54	19
Medium, 5-19.9	41	48	39	51
Large, 20 and above	7	35	7	30

SOURCE: Baljit Singh and Shridhar Misra, *A Study of Land Reforms in Uttar Pradesh* (Honolulu, 1964), tables 12 and 14.

tion of landlords did not do very much to change the basic structure of control of cultivation.

Seven percent of the cultivating households control 30 percent of the land cultivated. The actual control of land by a minority of relatively big cultivators is probably understated in Table 5 for various reasons. One is that since the survey was based on asking cultivators about their holdings, probably the bigger landholder understated his holdings, because he was afraid of having land taken away. A second reason is that at the time of landlord abolition, bigger holders resorted to a number of illegal devices to continue their control of the land. Unfortunately, Singh and Misra did not try to investigate this possibility. However, in a very careful study of the working of the Land Reform Act of 1953 in West Bengal, S. K. Basu and S. K. Bhattacharyya did set out to see how much land was transferred illegally to avoid the land ceilings placed by the act. They had to develop a series of indirect measures of these illegal transfers, but basically they studied the pattern of land transfers to relatives by sale or gift, but not by inheritance or division, the usual forms of land transfer among relatives. They studied the pattern of transfers for four years before and four years after the implementation of the act. They estimated that in the eight districts they studied, from 9 to 12 percent of the land transfers were to avoid the working of the act and that a total of more than 105,000 acres were held above the ceilings in the act. In 1953 it was estimated that there were 40,000 families holding about 400,000 acres above the land ceiling. Therefore, by a very conservative estimate, the large holders were able, through illegal means, to retain at least one-quarter of the lands they should have lost.[2] In 1954–1955 after the implementation of land reforms, the

2 S. K. Basu and S. K. Bhattacharyya, *Land Reforms in West Bengal: A Study on Implementation* (New Delhi, 1963), pp. 80–82.

Indian government carried out a sample survey of 4,456 villages through-out India to determine the structure of landholding and cultivation in rural India (see Table 6).

TABLE 6
Land ownership of rural households on a sample basis, 1953–1954

Kind of holding, acres		Percent of rural households	Percent of area owned
Small	0–1	47	1
	1–5	28	15
		75	16
Medium	5–20	19	41
Large	20 plus	6	43
		25	84

SOURCE: Government of India, Cabinet Secretariat, *The National Sample Survey*, Eighth Round, July 1954–April 1955, 66, Report on Land Holdings (4), Delhi Manager of Publications, 1962, 12.

Seventy-five percent of all rural households in the survey cultivated 5 acres or less, using a total of 16 percent of the land cultivated. Medium-sized cultivators, representing 19 percent of rural households, cultivated 41 percent of the land; and the 6 percent who could be considered large cultivators cultivated 43 percent of all the land.

Not all India's people who can be classified as rural are directly dependent on cultivation for their primary source of income. In a study of more than 8,500 rural households, the National Council of Applied Economic Research found that over 77 percent of the rural households in their sample were directly dependent on agriculture as their main source of income. In 2.5 percent of the households, there was no one gainfully employed by the criteria the surveyors used. More than 20 percent of rural households, therefore, derive their principal income from activities not directly involved in the production of agricultural products. These included self-employed business men, such as traders and craftsmen (10 percent of the households); nonagricultural wage earners engaged in things like construction and transportation (about 8.5 percent); and salary earners, such as teachers and minor government officials (1.5 percent).[3] In an intensive study of twelve small villages in eastern

[3] National Council of Applied Economic Research, *All India Rural Household Survey*, 2, *Income Investment and Savings* (New Delhi, 1965), tables 43 and 44.

Uttar Pradesh, Muhammad Shafi, a geographer, found that the percentage of the population directly dependent on agriculture ranged from 79 to 88 percent, with an average of 84 percent. The slight difference between the number of people directly dependent on agriculture in Shafi's study and that in the national survey is attributable to the small size of the villages in Shafi's sample, which would support fewer specialists than would larger villages included in the national sample.[4] In 1962 the National Council of Applied Economic Research conducted a survey of wealth and savings of over 8,000 households in India. It was found that 62 percent of all rural households had incomes below Rs. 1,200 a year, a little more than $200 a year on the basis of exchange rates in 1962. The agricultural wage earners (average income Rs. 765) and nonagricultural earners (average income Rs. 1,035), who account for 36 percent of rural households, are the poorest groups in the rural society, with 77 percent and 72 percent of the two groups, respectively, falling well below the line of average annual income. Self-employed farmers and salary earners, about 52 percent of rural households, were clearly better off.

There is a concentration of income in the top 10 percent of rural households, accounting for 33 percent of the total rural income, or an average of Rs. 3,500 a year; the bottom 10 percent get 2 percent of the income, or an average of Rs. 280 a year.[5]

The uneven concentration of income in rural society is replicated in the holding of tangible wealth, where, if anything, concentration is more intense than with income. The average tangible wealth of rural households is a little more than Rs. 1,000, or about $200. Seventy-six percent of rural households held less than this average amount, with one-third having assets of less than Rs. 200, or 3 percent of the total tangible wealth. The upper 10 percent of the households in the survey owned 55 percent of the wealth in rural society. The top 1 percent owned 18 percent of the wealth and had an average of Rs. 18,000 in assets.[6]

We can then say that India's 65.7 million rural households have the following economic characteristics. Ten percent of the households hold almost half of the land, with the upper 10 percent holding 55 percent of the tangible wealth and getting 33 percent of the rural income. The poverty of the bottom groups in rural society is even more striking than the wealth and income of the top groups. The bottom 75 percent own only 16 percent of the land; the bottom 10 percent in income gets only

[4] Muhammad Shafi, *Land Utilization in Eastern Uttar Pradesh* (Aligarh, 1960).

[5] National Council of Applied Economic Research, *All India Rural Household Survey*, 2 (1965), 19–32.

[6] *Ibid.*, pp. 29–38.

2 percent of the rural income; and the bottom third of the rural households owns only 3 percent of the tangible wealth in the countryside.
Therefore, the economic structure of the Indian countryside can be
described broadly as follows. At least one-third to one-half of its
population, who are very poor in comparison with the rest of rural society,
have little or no land, little tangible wealth, and little annual income; a
middle stratum, of perhaps 20 to 40 percent, have land income of about
Rs. 1,200 per year and about Rs. 1,000 worth of tangible property; a top
10 percent own half the land, over half the tangible wealth, and get
one-third the total of the rural segment of the economy.

LANGUAGE

Edmund Leach, an anthropologist, in discussing political and cultural
units in highland Burma, observed, "For a man to speak one language
rather than another is a ritual act, it is a statement about one's personal
status; to speak the same language as one's neighbours expresses soli-
darity with those neighbours, to speak a different language from one's
neighbours expresses social distance or even hostility." [7] The documenta-
tion of this statement can be seen repeatedly in past and present Indian
society. The internal political map of India since the early fifties has
been redrawn along linguistic boundaries. The attempt to use one Indian
language, Hindi, as the language of governmental administration and as
a national language has led to rioting and bloodshed, particularly in
southern India. The use of a regional language as the medium of in-
struction in colleges has made nonnative speakers of those regional
languages feel unwanted as teachers and students in the colleges. In
the past, languages or literary styles were associated with particular
religious or social groups. Braj Bhasa, a literary style that developed
in Uttar Pradesh several hundred years ago, for example, became the
medium for the spread of the poetry connected with the Krishna cult.
Avadhi, which developed in central Uttar Pradesh, spread orally through
Uttar Pradesh, as the language of Tulsi Das's *Ramayana*.

In the latter nineteenth century, Hindi, the language that has become
the official national language of India, was associated with the Arya
Samaj, a Hindu reform movement. In thinking about the languages of
India, where the census of 1961 recorded speakers of 1,018 different
languages, it is necessary to understand a series of linguistic and social
facts. A language, following Ferguson and Gumperz, "consists of all
varieties [of a language] which share a single superimposed variety
having substantial similarity in phonology and grammar with the in-

[7] E. R. Leach, *Political Systems of Highland Burma* (London, 1954), p. 49.

cluded varieties or which are mutually intelligible or are connected by a series of mutually intelligible varieties." [8] In Ferguson's terms, a variety may be a dialect or style of human speech patterns broad enough to function as a normal means of communication between two speakers. The superimposed variety, for example, is a literary standard. An American may have difficulty understanding the English spoken by a West Indian, whose native language is also English, or by an Indian who has learned it as a second language; but all three, if literate, can read the same issue of *The New York Times* or the *Manchester Guardian*, as all three share a standard literary language. The American, the West Indian, and the Indian all speak dialects of English. In thinking about languages in India, it is necessary to think horizontally, in terms of the distribution as mapped by a linguist of the varieties of the languages and the languages themselves. Mapping languages and dialects involves techniques of studying phonology, grammar, and vocabulary and tends to be seen in terms of the history of the languages and dialects.

Since the early twentieth century, when G. A. Grierson's *Linguistic Survey of India* was published, linguists have grouped the languages of India into four families: Indo-Aryan languages, spoken by almost 322 million, or 73.3 percent, of the people in India, mainly in northern and central India, and belonging to the same language family as European languages; Dravidian languages, spoken in southern India by more than 107 million, or 24.5 percent, of the Indian population (Dravidian is a language family found only in southern Asia); Tibeto-Chinese, related to Tibetan and the languages of northern southeastern Asia and spoken by 3.2 million people in the Himalayan fringe from Ladakh to eastern Assam; and Austro-Asiatic, spoken by tribals in the highland tribal belt of West Bengal, Bihar, Orissa, and Madhya Pradesh by 6.2 million, or 1.5 percent, of the Indian population. Austro-Asiatic languages are also found outside of India in southeastern Asia. Table 7 presents statistics on the major languages of India, based on the 1961 census of India.

The distribution of the language families in India is important for broad-scale reconstruction of the early cultural history of India. The presence of Tibeto-Burman speakers and their location in the northeast and the Himalayan fringe is a clear reflection of the ethnological connections of the peoples of this area to Tibet and southeastern Asia.

Asian peoples have been settled in these areas for long periods of time and have maintained their linguistic and cultural identity. There is

[8] Charles A. Ferguson and John J. Gumperz (eds.), "Linguistic Diversity in South Asia," *Indiana University Research Center in Anthropology, Folklore and Linguistics*, publication 13; also, part III, *International Journal of American Linguistics*, 26, 3 (July, 1960), 7.

TABLE 7

Languages in India, 1961

Indo-Aryan	574 languages	321,721,000 speakers	73.30% of total Indian population
Inner Subbranch		212,482,000	
*Hindi		133,435,000	
*Urdu		23,323,000	
*Gujarati		20,304,000	
Rajasthani		14,933,000	
*Punjabi		10,951,000	
Pahari		4,562,000	
Other		4,974,000	
Outer Subbranch		109,239,000	
*Bengali		33,889,000	
*Marathi		33,281,000	
Bihari		16,807,000	
*Orija		15,719,000	
*Assamese		6,803,000	
Other		3,199,000	
Dravidian	**153 languages**	**107,411,000 speakers**	**24.5% of total Indian population**
*Telugu		37,668,000	
*Tamil		30,563,000	
*Kannada		17,416,000	
*Malayam		17,016,000	
Other		4,749,000	
Austro-Asiatic	**65 languages**	**6,192,000 speakers**	**1.5% of total Indian population**
Santali		3,247,000	
Mundari		737,000	
Ho		648,000	
Other		1,560,000	
Tibeto-Chinese	**226 languages**	**3,184,000 speakers**	**0.7% of total Indian population**
Mainpuri		621,000	
Noga languages		478,000	
Garo		307,000	
Bodo		286,000	
Lushai		222,000	
Bhotia		207,000	
Other		1,063,000	

SOURCE: Census of India, 1961. Vol. I, Part II–C(ii), "Language Tables." Pp. ccxxx–ccxlii and pp. 33–76.

* Languages listed in Eighth Schedule of the Constitution.

evidence that Austric speakers were much more widespread during earlier times. Khasi, the language of the people of the Khasi Hills in Assam, is an Austric language. The bulk of the speakers of Austric languages in India, the Munda stock, with almost 6 million speakers, Ho, Santali, and Munda being the principal languages, are now concentrated in the highland tribal belt in southern Bengal Bihar, northwestern Orissa, and northeastern Madhya Pradesh. There is evidence that some of the scattered remnants of tribes in southern India may have been Austric speakers earlier. Linguists and anthropologists, combining this linguistic evidence with evidence from physical anthropology, speculate on the existence of a widespread Austric culture that flourished in India as well as southeastern Asia in prehistoric times.

Dravidian, which is now restricted to the southern third of the peninsula except for a pocket of Brahui, a Dravidian language spoken by several million people in Baluchistan in West Pakistan, was probably spoken all over India before the middle of the second millennium B.C. At this time, speakers of the fourth and largest language family began to enter India from the northwest. These peoples, now referred to as Aryans, spoke an Indo-European language, now called Sanskrit. The earliest records we have of Sanskrit come from the *Rg Veda*, whose earliest hymns are dated around 1200 B.C. The *Rg Veda* is a series of hymns of praise to various gods sung at the time of sacrifices. Incidental materials contained in the *Rg Veda* indicate that the culture of the Aryans at this period and to the early part of the first millennium B.C. was of cattle keepers who wandered over the plains of the Punjab and gradually settled down in villages to follow a sedentary agricultural existence. From the beginning of the first millennium, the Indo-Aryan speakers gradually spread down the Ganges Valley and to the southwest into central India and the peninsula. Probably after a period of bilingualism, the peoples of northern and central India who had been Dravidian speakers became speakers of Indo-Aryan languages.

Even the earliest Sanskrit recorded in the *Rg Veda* shows considerable influence of Austric and Dravidian languages, particularly in the adoption of a series of retroflex consonants, in verb structure, and in the adoption of a large number of words of Dravidian and Austric origin.[9]

Murray Emeneau, the linguist, calls India a linguistic area, by which he means an area that includes more than one language family, one of which, at least, spreads outside of the area, but one whose languages show features not found in the languages existing outside of the area.

---

[9] F. Burrow, *The Sanskrit Language* (London, 1955), pp. 377–88; Murray B. Emeneau, "Linguistic Pre-History of India," *Proceedings of the American Philosophical Society*, 98, 4 (1954), pp. 282–92; and "India as a Linguistic Area," *Language*, 32 (1956), 3–16.

Emeneau feels that "certainly the end result of the borrowings is that the languages of the two families, Indo-Aryan and Dravidian, seem in many respects more akin to one another than Indo-Aryan does to the other Indo-European languages." [10] There has been, of course, considerable borrowing from Indo-Aryan languages by Dravidian languages, particularly of lexical items, so that the vocabularies of the southern Indian languages, particularly Malayalam, have been heavily Sanskritized. The history of the relationships among the language families in India illustrates by analogy a general process in Indian civilization—that what appears on the surface as great and real diversity can be seen to have underlying connections, if not unity.

The later history of Sanskrit is important to an understanding of the nature and distribution of the northern Indian languages and also illustrates important cultural processes in the civilization. When the Aryans entered India sometime after 1500 B.C., they apparently spoke a number of dialects of a common language. One of these dialects became fixed for ritual purposes by 250 B.C. The priests of the Aryans and the Brahmans used it in writing down their religious literature. The language that became the medium of rituals was called polished, or the *Sanskrit*, to distinguish it from the natural language spoken by the people. By the fifth century, several main dialects or separate languages had developed, called the unpolished, or the *Prakrits*. One of these Prakrits was Pali, spoken in western India and later becoming the language of the Buddhists. Pali, too, started out as the language of the people, was used to reach the people for a religious reform movement, and finally became a frozen language for ritual purposes. The languages the people spoke continued to change through time, and a new level derived from the Prakrits began to merge by the second and third centuries—these were the *Apabhramsas*, the decayed or corrupt speech. It is from these languages that, by 1000, the modern Indo-Aryan vernaculars began to appear.

Modern Indo-Aryan languages are classified on phonemic and syntactical grounds into two main subbranches: an *outer subbranch* comprising Western Punjabi or Lahdna and Sindhi in the northwest, in what is now Pakistan, the *eastern southern subbranch* of Oriya, Bengali, Assamese, and Bhari, and the *southern subbranch* with Marathi; the *inner subbranch*, with Eastern and Western Hindi, Punjabi, Pahari, Rajasthani, and Gujarati. All these, with the exception of Eastern Hindi, share a common Apabhramsa, Nagara, as their ancestor. Eastern Hindi, which is spoken in the band running from the Himalayan foothills in eastern and central Uttar Pradesh down through the Vindhyas in Madhya Pradesh, descends from an Apabhramsa that has some similarities to

[10] Emeneau, *op. cit.* (1956), p. 16.

the ancestors of Bihari and Bengali. All the languages of the inner Indo-Aryan subbranch, with the exception of Gujarati, are associated territorially with *madhyadesha*, the heartland of classical India. Gujarati, the one inner subbranch language not found in this central territory, is spoken in an area that was conquered and colonized from the area around Delhi during the latter part of the first millennium.

A discussion of the historical distribution of the languages of India, although important to an understanding of the cultural history of India, obscures the social reality of language distribution in India today as well as in the past, that is, the function of language in communication and identification. The discussion of the distribution of the languages and their history is largely based on literary evidence relating to standardized forms of the language, either as recognized at the time by specialists or by criteria regarding syntax, morphology, and phonemics of the language as understood by modern scholars, and does not necessarily tell all we need to know about the actuality of spoken communication at any particular moment.

Anthropological linguists like John Gumperz, William Bright, and William McCormack have developed a different picture of the distribution of languages and dialects as they actually exist on the "ground" in India. Any village, it has been found, has a local village speech used in a very narrow geographic range. The Indo-Aryan languages of northern India can be seen at the village level as a series of gradually changing speech varieties with no breaks along the chain from village to village in terms of communication. If, however, a villager speaking only his local dialect goes 100 miles in either direction, his ability to communicate with villagers of the place he is visiting is greatly impaired. Coexistent with local village dialects are several other kinds of supra-local or superimposed styles or dialects. When the villager goes to the nearby town or bazaar and deals with traders or merchants, he may speak a regional dialect that has a much wider spread than the local village dialect. At various times within a region, a dialect becomes standardized through use for ritual or literary purposes, and so a literature develops. There are many examples of such regional standard dialects—Braj in western Uttar Pradesh, Maithli in Bihar, Chattigarhi in Madhya Pradesh. Very often these regional dialects were associated with persistent political centers.[11]

[11] John J. Gumperz, "Language Problems in the Rural Development of North India," *Journal of Asian Studies*, 16 (1957), 251–59. John J. Gumperz and C. M. Naim, "Formal and Informal Standards in the Hindi Regional Language Area" in Charles A. Ferguson and John J. Gumperz, "Linguistic Diversity in South Asia," *International Journal of American Linguistics*, 26, 3 (July 1960), 92–118.

In the last 150 years there have developed, and become relatively fixed, regional standard languages, such as Bengali, Tamil, Marathi, and Hindi. These are learned in school, spoken in the major urban centers, and used for region-wide literary, administrative, and social purposes. Today these regional standards usually have two versions, a spoken and a written form. Pillai, a linguist and native speaker of Tamil, describes language styles of an educated Tamilian:

Literary Tamil is the one he employs in classroom lectures, in public meetings, and on certain other formal occasions. The vocabulary of this latter style corresponds to his writing in journals. The pronunciation is similar to that of the all-India Radio news broadcasts in Tamil and to that ordinarily employed in reading a written text. The colloquial Tamil is the one he uses in ordinary conversation, when talking to his family and friends and also to students outside the classroom. It is similar to the style employed by other educated native Tamils throughout the present Madras State, but differs from the speech of the uneducated. The dialects used by the latter show a number of regional and caste variations.[12]

The standardization of the regional languages was given great impetus by the establishment of printing in the eighteenth century, and wide-scale dissemination of published materials during the nineteenth and twentieth centuries. When books and newspapers began to be published, their writers essentially established norms for "proper" usage and vocabulary that were incorporated into textbooks and other literary materials. Very often, as with Fort William College, in Calcutta, established by the British to train their administrators in the languages of India, or with missionaries who wanted to translate and publish the Bible for use in converting the Indian people to Christianity, small groups of Indians worked with the Europeans in establishing the standard for the regional language. Bengali, the language established as the regional language in the early nineteenth century, was heavily Sanskritized both in grammar and vocabulary and was far removed from any of the spoken dialects. At the same time, the Bengali dialect actually spoken by educated Bengalis in Calcutta became established as the regional standard for educated Bengali throughout Bengal, but the spoken regional standard and the written literary standard were almost two different languages in the nineteenth century.[13]

[12] M. Shanmugam Pillai, "Tamil-Literary and Colloquial," in Charles Ferguson and John J. Gumperz (eds.), "Linguistic Diversity in South Asia," *International Journal of American Linguistics,* 26, 3 (July, 1960), 27.

[13] Edward C. Dimock, "Literary and Colloquial Bengali in Modern Bengali Prose," in Charles A. Ferguson and John J. Gumperz (eds.), "Linguistic Diversity in South Asia," *International Journal of American Linguistics,* 26, 3 (July, 1960), 43–63.

The history of the languages known today as Hindi and Urdu, and formerly as Hindustani, is quite complicated but illustrates a general process of language development in relation to Indian cultural and political history. When the Islamic invaders had established themselves in northern India, they learned the regional dialect spoken to the north and northeast of Delhi in the present districts of Meerut and Moradabad. This language was used and spread by soldiers, traders, and administrators, and became the *lingua franca* through much of northern India, and was carried into the south with the Muslims, so that even speakers of Dravidian languages who wanted or had to deal with the conquerors learned it. This language came to be called Urdu, the language of the camp, and incorporated a large number of Persian-derived words, because Persian was the administrative language of the conquerors. By the seventeenth century and particularly in the eighteenth century, a process had developed that we see repeatedly in the linguistic history of India. What started as a dialect or *lingua franca* then developed a stylized literary form, particularly for poetry, which became highly Persianized, fixed, and quite far removed from the actual spoken version of the language. The spoken and literary styles were used by both Hindus and Muslims. In the eighteenth century, Urdu was written in the Arabic-Persian script. In the nineteenth century, it became the Indian language of the lower courts and lower levels of the administration in northern India, replacing Persian, which had been the official Indian language for administration until 1835. In the higher levels of the courts and administrative system, English was the official language. At the same time, from the impetus partially of the British and then increasingly of Hindu reformers in northern India, a different version, using Devanagri, the Sanskrit-derived script, came into use by Hindus for educational and other purposes. This version was called Hindi. In the development of nineteenth- and twentieth-century Hindi, Sanskrit-derived words began to replace words of Persian and Arabic origin, that were associated with the conquest of India by the Muslims. The spoken version, usually called Hindustani, remained the same until 1947, so that some people who claimed to be speaking Urdu in reality were speaking the same language.

Today, one can travel over most of northern India and find speakers of Hindi ranging from illiterate coolies or rickshaw pullers in Bombay, a Marathi- and Gujarati-speaking city, in Calcutta, a Bengali-speaking city, in Delhi, the original Hindi-speaking area, to highly educated professionals. In the cities, many have learned Hindi as a means of communication even if they speak a regional language. As more and more of the educated classes move about from city to city and from town to town, they tend to have their children learn standard Hindi instead of their regional language if they come from an area in which the sub-regional language is related to Hindi or as a second language if their regional language is, for example, Bengali or Marathi. Educated speakers of Hindi, Punjabi, Rajasthani, and Bihari have all accepted standard Hindi or *Khari Boli*, the "standing language," in addition to their local dialect (*dihati*, of the village) and their regional languages. Many urban workers, even in Bengal and Bombay, tend to speak an uneducated version of Khari Boli as well as their *dihati*. Traveled and educated speakers of other Indo-Aryan languages, such as Marathi and Bengali, often speak some Hindi to communicate with their servants and with those whom they supervise in work situations or as a result of having traveled in northern India.

The census of India records 133,435,000 persons who speak Hindi and 23,323,000 who speak Urdu as their mother tongue. It is difficult to know whether all the speakers recorded under these two language categories do speak the same language. Probably, because of the village dialects that are counted as part of Hindi or Urdu, they, in fact, do not. On the other hand, the actual number of speakers of Khari Boli is increasing through the spread of education and the prestige that at least in northern India adheres to Khari Boli. The census of 1961 states that those who report Hindi as their mother tongue consist of three groups: those whose mother tongue is structurally akin to Khari Boli in that they speak one of the dialects of Western Hindi; those who have adopted as their colloquial language the literary form, now the official language of administration and used in business offices and schools; and, finally, those whose mother tongue is in reality outside of the Western Hindi dialect area, such as Eastern Hindi or Bihari, but who speak Khari Boli almost as an associated mother tongue and who, for reasons of prestige, claim their mother tongue to be a variety of Khari Boli.[14] Geographically, there are three levels in any major language in India— a local dialect; a subregional dialect, which may or may not have a standardized literary and spoken form; and a regional standard with both a literary and a colloquial form.

In addition to these three levels, since the first millennium B.C., India has always had one or more languages that could be used widely throughout the civilization. Sanskrit for 3,000 years has been the medium for religious communication. From the twelfth to the early nineteenth century, Persian was the language for most official activities; and, for some Hindus and Muslims, it was the language of polite society and literary communication. Urdu or Bazaar Hindustani was a *lingua franca*

[14] *Census of India, 1961*, I, part II–cii, "Language" Tables, cciii.

for commercial purposes. Since the beginning of the nineteenth century, the English language provided a means of communication for educated groups throughout society. There is no reliable way of estimating how many people speak, read, and understand English in India today, but it certainly would be in excess of 15 million. Over fifty English language daily newspapers have a combined circulation of more than 1 million. If one thinks of the millions of college and high school graduates, most of whom at least read and understand English, one gets some idea of the spread of English as a second or third language for people in India. Finally, since Independence, although the increase of the use of Hindi has not been so rapid as its advocates desired when they framed the Constitution in 1949, in northern India it is widely used and understood even by primary school graduates. Thus far, in the discussion of languages, we have been talking about the horizontal spread of languages and their distribution. By implication, though, it should be clear that there is a social-situational component to the languages people use. Recent research demonstrates not only that a dialect is found in a particular place but that groups in the same place use different dialects. Throughout much of northern India there are distinct dialect differences between the upper castes and the untouchables in a particular village. These dialect differences are not enough to prevent communication but do indicate a social separation of the two groups. In southern India, research indicates that often there are three broad social dialects—one for Brahmans, one for so-called non-Brahmans, and still another for Untouchables.

How a person speaks and what he says mark him socially; certain kinds of speech are appropriate in certain situations. A highly educated Western-trained scientist working in a major city uses in his work and in discussion with his colleagues English or a mixture of the regional standard and English. Very often conversations, particularly regarding work situations, have the grammatical form of the regional standard with many nouns in English. At home he uses the colloquial version of the regional standard, or, perhaps, if his wife is not educated, the subregional language is spoken. When he returns to his village, he uses the *dihati*, the local dialect of the village, even when speaking with people as highly educated as himself. Very often, to a linguist or an outsider, the regional standard that this scientist uses in the city, the version of the regional standard or the subregional language he uses at home, and his village dialect are as distinct as three different languages; but this scientist is not fully aware of the magnitude of the differences in his own speech. In doing anthropological field work in a village in eastern Uttar Pradesh, I found that the village dialect used by the villagers was derived from an Apabhramsa that separated from the ancestor of modern standard Hindi in the tenth century. The village dialect and standard Hindi are not mutually intelligible, but educated people in the village, as well as others who speak both the village dialect and standard Hindi, thought of the two languages as being the same, one the spoken form (*Dihati*) and the other its written form (*Khari Boli*).

Religious and social situations have particular languages associated with them. Even at local political meetings, the regional standard is used, with the result that many in the audience get only the drift of what is being said. Particular religious performances, such as *kirtans*, performances of devotional songs, are sung in Uttar Pradesh in one of the subregional languages. The *Ramayana*, which is performed as a play during a festival, is in another subregional language. If it were otherwise, it would not meet the cultural expectations of the audience and the participants. The direction in language change in India today is clear. Gradually, particularly as there is a spread of education and literacy, as there is increasing geographic mobility in society, as the administration of development and welfare plans reach farther and wider into the countryside, the regional standards will become more and more widely used and understood. The possibility, though, of the development of an all-India language that is widely understood seems much less likely, and India will probably continue, as it has been for millennia, as a multilanguage civilization, in which communication has frequently been along chains of speakers or readers rather than directly, face-to-face, through one language.

CHAPTER FIVE

The Shaping of the Civilization:
Views of the Past

We have looked at the geography of southern Asia and its influence on the cultures and societies in the subcontinent, the present economic structure, the distribution of the peoples, and the languages of India. Throughout this discussion, especially of cultural geography and languages, the past is crucial to understanding the present. It is often said that Hindus do not have a historical sense. What is meant by this statement is that Hindus do not have a conception of history concerned with exact chronology and with establishing accuracy through documentary study, nor a long-range theory of historical causality based on the accidental juxtaposition of events. Hindus and all Indians, however, are very much aware of their past and have a vigorous sense of the past, if not of history as we in the West have come to define it in the last 200 years.

India has a segmented civilization—segmented by region, by major religious tradition, and by position within the social hierarchy—where one's place and social position are determined, to some extent, and determined the kind of past that one refers to. It is useful to think of two kinds of past that an Indian may have: a ritual, mythological past and a direct, social-political past. The mythic-ritual past relates people to the great traditions of India, providing sacred ties that justify or explain the situations people find themselves in. Throughout much of northern India one finds a group called Rajputs, who today claim to be the descendants of members of the second great order of society, the Kshatriyas. Their past goes back to the *Ramaycna* and the *Mahabharata*, great epics of the late first millennium B.C., which tell of warfare connected with the spread of Sanskritic civilization over the subcontinent. These epics set a moral code of respect, acceptance, and carrying out of one's duty; present the supernatural as concerned with and intervening in human affairs; and exalt action above contemplation. The past of the present-day Rajput of northern India is embodied in and conveyed to him through a mythic past dramatized in an annual performance of events from the life of Rama, the hero of the *Ramayana*. At the time of *Dasahra*, the autumnal equinox, in many of the towns and villages in northern India, parts of the *Ramayana* of Tulsi Das, or the *Ramacaritamanas,* are chanted and acted out for large audiences. Every year, Rama, the hero, is de-frauded of his rightful patrimony as king of Ayodhya; his faithful and pure wife, Sita, is abducted by the villain; and Rama and his younger brother, Laksmana, set off over much of India in pursuit. In their travels they meet demons and, aided by holy men and common people and finally in alliance with the king of the monkeys, Hanuman, cross to Ceylon and defeat Ravana, the villain. In the play, the *Ram Lila,* Ravana and his brother Kumbhakarna, are represented by large paper and bam-boo effigies, often 15 or 20 feet high, which are burned on the last night of the *Ram Lila,* the drama cycle. The next day, in the final scene, Rama, Sita, and Lakshmana return to Ayodha, and the audience, in effect, be-comes the citizens of the town to welcome Rama back; and, amidst the playing of bands, all join in the cry of victory to Rama, "Jai Ram."

Although all groups in the society attend and, to this extent, par-ticipate in the *Ram Lila,* it is the Rajputs who identify most clearly with the drama and message. They claim descent from Rama; often their names come from the *Ramayana.* A good wife is referred to as Sita, events in the village are compared with events in the *Ramayana,* and actions are explained or justified on the basis of the stories learned from the presentation of the *Ram Lila.*[1]

The mythological past is communicated in other large-scale corporate performances and rituals at different times, in different places, and with different contents, for example, the *Durga Puja,* celebrated in Bengal to memorialize the victory of the goddess Durga over the buffalo-headed demon Mahishasur. Much of the *Durga Puja* is a household celebration, but increasingly there are musical performances, dancing, and theater connected with it, at which large crowds assemble. The past is also main-tained and transmitted in less spectacular cultural performances than

[1] For a discussion of the *Ramayana,* the *Ramacaritamas,* and the *Ram Lila,* see W. Douglas P. Hill, *The Holy Lake of the Acts of Rama: An English Translation of Tulsai Das's Ramacaritamanas* (Oxford, 1952), and Norvin Hein, "The Ram Lila," in Milton Singer (ed.), *Traditional India: Structure and Change* (Philadelphia, 1959), pp. 73–98.

the *Ram Lila* and the *Durga Puja:* recitations, formal gatherings to hear stories, religious sings or *bhajans,* attendance at temples, and films of a kind well known in India called "mythologicals," relating to the past of India.

The past is also embodied in local traditions that may be maintained through genealogies of particular families, lineages, and segments of castes or through stories told by genealogies (Bhats) and family Brahmans. When a Hindu goes on a pilgrimage to a sacred place, he usually contacts priests who traditionally serve his ancestors at that sacred shrine. As Vidyarthi tells us in his description of Gaya, an important sacred center where many Hindus go to perform rituals connected with death, the Gayawal, priests of Gaya, maintain books of genealogical information on all their clients. Not only does the client come to the priest, but the priest or his representative visits the client at his home, taking with him his attendants, musicians, and sacred objects, performing various rituals, and recounting events from the mythic past.[2]

For many lower castes, the view of the past embodied in their myths and stories accounts for their present degraded or low position. Most caste-origin myths of the lower castes involve a mishap, an act of greed, or an accident, usually in connection with actions aimed at defending sacred honor, which caused the downfall from a higher status. For example, some Chamars, an untouchable caste of northern India, tell the story of four Brahman brothers who were one day walking by the side of a river and saw a cow stuck in the mud. They tried various things to get her out, and then, as one of the brothers was tugging at the tail of the cow, she died. Because he was touching the cow at the moment of her death, he became implicated in the death; and from then on, the descendants of this Brahman became the Chamars who are relegated to a very low position and, among other things, traditionally have to remove the carcasses of dead animals, considered highly polluting. The myth explains to the Chamars their degraded position in the present social system but also allows them to claim a higher status, since they once had been of the Brahman order in society.

In a village or town, a casual question or observation on a building or ruin brings a flood of historical reminiscences. A query about who

<hr />

[2] L. P. Vidyarthi, *The Sacred Complex in Hindu Gaya* (London, 1961). For discussion of ritual performances and their significance for maintaining tradition in the modern urban setting, see Milton Singer, "The Great Tradition in a Metropolitan Center: Madras," in Milton Singer (ed.), *Traditional India: Structure and Change* (Philadelphia, 1959), pp. 141–82. On genealogists, see A. M. Shah and R. G. Shroff, "The Vahivanca Barots of Gujarat: A Caste of Genealogists and Mythographers," in Singer (ed.), *op. cit.,* pp. 40–70.

owns a piece of land leads to a genealogy and a story of warfare and conquest that establishes the person's right to the land. Direct historical stories justify, explain, and maintain the social structure and relationships. Alliances or enmities at the formal level in a village are often maintained over generations, the present relationship being explained by the past. I knew two very good friends in a village of the same caste and lineage who would not eat at each other's house on formal ritual occasions, because three or four generations before there had been a fight between two ancestors leading to a house burning. The formal enmity established at that time is still symbolized by the two households' bar against interdining between their members. Corporate groups appear under some circumstances to be able to maintain a historical identity through long periods of time. The Saurathas are a silk-weaving community found in Madurai in Madras, but they continue to identify with their ancient home in Gujarat. At the time of a marriage, the bridegroom's family goes to claim the bride at her house, and when they are questioned as to who they are, they respond by reciting the history of their caste.

The past for an Indian, then, is a living past that can be recalled for an individual or a group in a ritual or nonritual context, attaching him to large groups and to the civilization through a widespread mythic past or tying him to a limited group and to one place.

During the last 100 years another kind of past has been developing and is becoming widely known. Individuals and groups within society have been formulating, codifying, and diffusing a past and views of the past more akin to the kind of past that modern Americans and Europeans have—one which is identified, not with a social segment or a region, but with a nation and the people in the nation conceived of as a unit. Nationalist leaders from the end of the nineteenth century until the present have grasped the fact that political nationhood is connected with a cultural unity and a unified past not characteristic of Indian civilization, with its manifold traditions and regional and local variations. The development of a vigorous national past owes much to Bankim Chandra Chatterji, writer of nationalist-oriented historical novels, who stated the case for a new Indian history:

There is no Hindu history. Who will praise our noble qualities if we do not praise them ourselves? It is a rule of life that a man who does not let it be known that he is great is considered of no account by his fellows. When has the glory of any nation even been proclaimed by another nation? The proof of the warlike prowess of the Romans is to be found in Roman histories. The story of the heroism of the Greeks is contained in Greek writings. The case for Mussulman valour in battle rests only in their own records. The Hindus have no such glorious qualities simply because there is no written evidence.[3]

B. G. Tilak, one of the important early nationalists, attempted to make Shivaji, a seventeenth-century Maratha political and military leader into the prototype of the Indian freedom fighter and to establish a series of observances and public rituals that would glorify the Indian past and Shivaji. In 1893, Tilak along with a religious leader revived a household festival devoted to the god Ganesh and turned it into a public festival with clear nationalistic and anti-Muslim undertones. Shortly after the establishment of the Ganapati festival, Tilak and his followers established a festival to honor the great Maratha chief, Shivaji. The form of the celebration was that of a typical Hindu rite with readings from Sanskrit literature, distribution of *prasad,* offerings in the form of sweets, and processions. In addition, there were ballads glorifying Shivaji and lectures on Shivaji and Maratha history. The final act of the Shivaji festival was the carrying of Shivaji's portrait up to the mountain on which his monument stone had been erected.[4]

The revived Ganapati and the Shivaji festivals successfully drew large public support for a time, and they did help establish a nationalist identity for the people of Maharashtra; however, they did not spread widely to other regions, because the past invoked, and the heroes and events glorified, tended to be tied to one region.

Tilak and Aurobindo Ghose, another early nationalist, attempted with considerable success to select from the Hindu tradition concepts and ideals that could be reworked into religious cultural-national ideology. They reinterpreted the *Bhagavad-Gita,* which forms a small part of the *Mahabharata,* into an authoritative expression of Hindu thought. Tilak and Ghose independently used the *Gita* to justify political activism. They argued that it was the Hindu's *dharma,* religious duty, to further nationalism; by implication they argued, on the basis of their interpretation of the *Gita,* that violence was justified in a righteous cause and nationalism was a religiously given righteous cause. Gandhi also used the *Gita* as his basic religious text and derived from it a counterdoctrine of nonviolence. He interpreted the battle in the *Gita* as a metaphor standing for men's souls. How successful these two varying interpretations of the

[3] Quoted in T. W. Clark, "The Role of Bankimcandra in the Development of Nationalism," in C. H. Philips (ed.), *Historians of India, Pakistan and Ceylon* (London, 1961), p. 436.

[4] See Stanley Wolpert, *Tilak and Gokhale: Revolution and Reform in the Making of Modern India* (Berkeley, 1962), pp. 67–82, and Victor Barnouw, "The Changing Character of a Hindu Festival," *American Anthropologist,* 56 (1964), 74–86.

Gita were in helping mobilize mass support for the nationalist movement is an open question. The result, however, in terms of the establishment of the *Gita* as a kind of Hindu "bible," as the one holy book exalted over all the other religious texts, has been well established.[5]

The effort to establish a single past, a single tradition, and a single cultural identity with one nation and one people has generally proved unsuccessful in India. The use of Hindu heroes and symbolism exacerbated hostilities between Hindus and Muslims in the pre-Independence era and played a part in the 1947 partition of India, into India and Pakistan. India, established as a secular state at Independence, carefully chose non-Hindu symbols for its flag, which has the Buddhist Wheel of Law on it. The new government selected the Asokan lions as the national seal, Asoka being a Buddhist ruler; as the national anthem, they rejected *Bandre Mataram*, which evokes the mother goddess, a Hindu deity, and which has, because of its origin in one of Bankichandras novels, an anti-Muslim flavor, in favor of a poem by Tagore, *Jana Gana Mana*, which is a listing of the regions and peoples of India.

Today, the Indian government tries very hard to develop a public history built around what is termed the "First War of Indian Independence," the Sepoy Mutiny of 1857, and the nationalist struggle of the twentieth century. The Mutiny or rebellion of 1857, however, touched only a third of the people of India at the time, and even the greatest and most revered of recent Indian leaders, Gandhi, is anathema to many people of India. The recent border wars with China in 1962 and with Pakistan in 1965 have been more productive, at least momentarily, of a sense of national identity on the part of the Indian people than any other recent events. The government was careful to elevate to the rank of hero, in both recent outbreaks of hostilities with neighbors, representatives of all communities: Hindus, Muslim Sikhs, and even Anglo-Indians.

There has been some success in the effort to form a unified Indian tradition among the educated classes who share a somewhat common view of the past and of their civilization. To some extent, Nehru, Prime Minister of India from 1946 to 1964, was the clearest exponent and, in his thought and writings, the embodiment of the "new Indian tradition." This view of India and its traditions as reinterpreted by a modern, secular, rationalist, political leader can best be seen in Nehru's effort at

---

[5] See Minoo Adenwalla, "Hindu Concepts and the Gita in Early National Thought," in Robert K. Sakai (ed.), *Studies on Asia* (Lincoln, Nebraska: University of Nebraska Press, 1961). For the whole question of the establishment of traditions for new states, see McKim Marriott, "Cultural Policy in the New States," in Clifford Geertz (ed.), *Old Societies and New States* (New York: Free Press, 1963), pp. 27–56.

personal history and exploration of his own intellectual position and part in history, *The Discovery of India*, written while he was in prison for his nationalist activities between 1942 and 1945, and published in 1946. Nehru asks in this book, "What is this India, apart from her physical and geographical aspects? What did she represent in the past? What gave her strength then? How did she lose that old strength, and has she lost it completely? Does she represent anything vital now, apart from being the home of a vast number of human beings?" [6]

Nehru saw India in the context of world history. He saw it partially through his own eyes, in traveling over India and meeting thousands of Indians, addressing thousands of meetings while preaching nationalism, and in fighting for Indian independence; he also saw it through the eyes of many Western scholars who interpreted Indian traditions for Western audiences. His concern with the past was to find that which he thought of as quintessentially Indian, which, in terms of process, was "unity in diversity," the ability to absorb and reshape that which came into India as foreign. Indian thought, both at the higher philosophical reaches and at the level of the peasant, accepts, Nehru believed, the idea that there is an order in the universe that functions according to law. Within this order, the individual has freedom to shape his own destiny. "There is belief in rebirth and an emphasis on unselfish love and disinterested activity. Logic and reason are relied upon and used effectively for argument, but it is recognized that often intuition is greater than either." [7]

Nehru basically accepted the view, developed in the nineteenth century by some Indians as a defense of their civilization against Western political and cultural domination, that India was strong in things of the spirit and the mind and that the West was strong in technology and materialistic goals. Nehru saw, as do most Indians today, British conquest and subjugation as an expression of the West's materialist civilization. India was, in this view, at a weak point politically and morally, a situation brought about largely by the effects of another foreign rule, that of the Muslims. While India was at its weakest, the British conquered it and, partially through design, partially through accident, destroyed much of the inherent balance of Indian life. Through exploiting India as a market, the British destroyed Indian craftsmen and kept India as an agricultural colony to supply raw materials for British industry. This led to rapid unemployment and poverty. This picture assumes

[6] Jawaharlal Nehru, *The Discovery of India* (N.Y.: The John Day Company, Inc., 1946), p. 37.
[7] *Ibid.*, pp. 175–76.

that the Indian people were relatively well off before their exploitation by the British and that it was British rule that led to stagnation in agriculture and the underdevelopment of modern industry in India.

Many modern educated Indians, then, see India as a great civilization that reached an apex or a classical period in the fifth and sixth centuries. This was a time of great literature and religious thought; India had produced two great world religions, Hinduism and Buddhism; Indians had made great contributions in astronomy and mathematics; they had developed a state system they now view as relatively benign and containing a republican component. From the sixth to the eighteenth century, this civilization, although not advancing rapidly, nonetheless showed great persistence. By and large, the civilization was able to come to terms with Islam, both culturally and socially. Great art forms evolved, particularly sculpture, and later, under the Muslims, painting. A balanced economy also evolved, centered around self-sufficient village communities which were immune to the political vicissitudes of the Muslim states and in which men had their place as farmers or craftsmen. This view of the Indian village in the nineteenth century was idealized and considered a kind of corporate democracy. The rigidities of the caste system and the degraded status of women, which grew partially as a defense against Islam and the efforts made to convert Hindus to Islam were interpreted as a fall from a previously more flexible and democratic society. The Mughal Empire, particularly under the Emperor Akbar (1556–1605), who followed a policy of religious toleration and political accommodation to Hindus, is seen, in this view of the past, as a period of synthesis when the Turkish invaders became Indianized and the many elite groups in India became Persianized. The last of the Great Mughal rulers, Aurangzib (1658–1707), reverted to an earlier Muslim attitude toward Hindus and India and attempted to push a militant Muslim Empire into southern India. He broke the political alliance between Hindu and Muslim and the cultural synthesis that emerged under Akbar. The dislocations attendant on the breakup of the Mughal Empire caused by Aurangzib's expansion and narrow cultural policies set the stage for British conquest and the exploitation of India in the nineteenth and early twentieth centuries.

The resurgence of India in the late nineteenth and twentieth centuries is seen as a reaction to British rule and the changes brought about in its wake. British government and European missionaries in India established schools in the English language medium, although this was done as an act of European arrogance exemplified in Lord Macaulay's statement, "a single shelf of a good European Library was worth the whole native literature of India and Arabia." The aim was also to provide semieducated

English-speaking clerks to man the lower levels of the British government in India. Many Indians, although distrustful of British motives in establishing a higher education system on the British model, see the access to Western rational thought and to Western social and political ideologies as being crucial to the reform of Indian society, particularly of Hinduism. Ram Mohan Roy (1772–1833), Keshub Sen (1838–1884), Swami Vivekananda (1863–1902), among others, are thought to have reformed Hinduism and Hindu thought, returning it to the Vedic simplicity of the first millennium B.C. Above all, these reformers and others led the fight to rid Hinduism of the social accretions of caste, sati, and the subjugation of women.

Structurally, the British, while fossilizing much of Indian social structure by their support of the princes and large landholders whom they created and maintained as a prop to their imperialistic rule, also provided the milieu in which a small but significant middle class grew up. Many members of this middle class are dismissed as "brown sahibs," who worked for the British and aped their styles and customs; but others provided the leadership for the nationalist struggle, which, under Gandhi and through the force of his benign, spiritual personality, tapped the soul of India and drew its great support from the mass of the Indian people as well as the Western-educated elite. This mass movement, under Gandhi's leadership and using his nonviolent methods, won India its freedom, which, though marred by the establishment of Pakistan, demonstrates the strength and character of the Indian people.

This is the rough picture, something of a caricature, which many educated Indians carry with them today. It is built onto and is slowly penetrating the myriad other kinds of past, direct and mythological, carried by the bulk of the Indian population. How rapidly this new total view of *the* Indian tradition and *the* Indian past will supplant other local pasts is a matter of conjecture. It is clearly tied to the spread of literacy, education, and mass communications as well as to the maintenance of a unitary political system in the present nation-state of India.

CHAPTER SIX

The Cultural and Structural History of India: Hindu Beginnings and Islamic Penetrations

In one sense, present-day Indian society and culture are the result of 5,000 years of Indian history stretching back to the Indus Valley cities of Harrapa and Mohenjodaro (300 to 1500 B.C.). Many now believe that the Indus Valley peoples were the ancestors of the Dravidian speakers and that the invading Indo-Aryan speakers were not the carriers of higher civilization into the subcontinent, as nineteenth-century Europeans tend to argue.

By the sixth century B.C., the Punjab and the Ganges Valleys were under cultivation, although there were large forest tracts interspersed or on the margins. People of the valley lived in settled village communities. Beyond the villages there were loose political organizations that were tribal. Often there was a tribal chief who was essentially a war leader, influenced if not controlled by the *sabha,* an assembly of elders or leaders or segments of the tribes, and the *samiti,* a body that appears to have represented wider groups, perhaps all adult males of the tribe.

When the Indo-Aryan-speaking peoples entered India around 1500 B.C., like their counterparts on the Iranian plateau, they were loosely divided into three orders of society: warriors, priests, and common people. By the sixth century the social ideology of the Indo-Aryan–speaking peoples was being obviously influenced if not shaped by their contacts with the non-Indo-Aryan agriculturalists and town dwellers already existing in India. By the third century B.C., there had crystallized a social ideology that divided society into four major orders (*varnas*): priests (the Brahmans), warriors (the Kshatriyas), traders (Vaishyas), and the cultivators (Shudras).

60

After discussing the creation of the universe at the time of the sacrifice of the god Prajapati, who was thought of as a primeval man, one of the late hymns of the *Rg Veda* presents the mythological charter for the establishment of the four orders of ancient Indian society:

> When they divided the Man,
>> into how many parts did they divide him?
> What was his mouth, what were his arms,
>> what were his thighs and his feet called?

> The Brahman was his mouth
>> of his arms was made the warrior
> His thighs became the vaisya
>> of his feet the sudra was born.[1]

Even after 200 years of textual scholarship, little can be said definitively about the relationship of the *varna* social ideology and the cluster of practices and institutions termed the caste system, which is characteristic of later Hindu Indian society. Nineteenth-century scholars sought the origin of the caste system in a racial conflict between the fair-skinned invading Indo-Aryans or Aryans and the darker indigenous peoples, the *Dasas* or *Dasyus*. They are unflatteringly described in the *Vedas* as flat-nosed and bull-lipped; they are worshipers of the phallus and speakers of an alien language; they are, however, fort or town dwellers as well as agriculturalists and cattle keepers; they are capable of organizing large military operations against the Indo-Aryans. Today, most scholars agree that the *Dasas* represent the Dravidian peoples, who were probably the descendants of the Indus Valley peoples and clearly had a more highly developed society and economy than the invading Indo-Aryans. Nineteenth-century European scholars and British administrators attributed their own feelings of racial superiority to the Indo-Aryans, saw them as the bearers of civilization to the Indians, and saw the caste system as the Indo-Aryans' effort to keep themselves aloof and racially pure by relegating the *Dasas* to the lower orders of society and prohibiting marriage with them.

The *varna* categories do not account for the fifth order in Indian society, the Untouchables or depressed or scheduled castes, who today include about 15 percent of the Indian population. If indeed the caste system had its origins in the Indo-Aryans' belief in the need to maintain racial and cultural exclusiveness from the indigenous peoples of India, one would assume that this could be demonstrated through the findings

[1] Quoted from A. L. Basham, *The Wonder that Was India* (London, 1954), p. 241.

of physical anthropology. A good deal of effort during the last seventy years has gone into measuring head forms, stature, breadth of the nose, and in more recent years, in trying to map the distribution of blood types in India. The best that can be said of this effort is that the findings are inconclusive. Some of the tribal peoples do have a different distribution of blood types from that of the Hindus and Muslims in the surrounding areas. There might be slight differences in distribution of blood types between upper-caste Hindus and Untouchables in particular regions.[2] However, even the differences in distribution of blood types within India, when viewed on the broader canvas of Asia and the world, indicate that no matter what their historical origin, the peoples within India are more like each other than like people outside.[3] Therefore, if the social ideology of the Indo-Aryans did include ideas of racial exclusiveness, they appear not to have been very successful in affecting the actual racial composition of Indian society.

The origins of the caste system are undoubtedly very complex, and its direct history will probably never be known. No single theory—be it race prejudice; the manipulation of small groups in the society, such as Brahmans who wanted to buttress an exclusive social position; differential valuation of occupations, which led to the valuing of some occupations and the despising of others; attempts of some groups within society to maintain their culture in the face of outside pressures; or the development of the idea of pollution and power, which led to fear of loss of power if one had contact with the food or body wastes of another group—has accounted for the origin of the system. None of the single causal theories has proved satisfactory, and today most anthropologists and sociologists feel it is fruitless to spend much time in trying to find the origins or trace the history of the caste system to its beginnings.

In the middle of the first millennium B.C., the society and culture of the Indo-Aryans, as shaped in the Indian environment, do not seem to have been so different from those of their distant relations in Iran and the eastern Mediterranean basin. Their original religious ideas, centered on the worship of sky gods through large-scale public and household sacrifices, had begun to incorporate earth deities and to become more concerned with agriculture. They had begun to develop a much more sophisticated religiophilosophical system and had acquired groups of ritual specialists concerned not only with the performance of sacrifice but with the development and maintenance of speculative religious

[2] See D. N. Majumdar, *Races and Cultures of India* (New York, 1961), pp. 25–121.

[3] William C. Boyd, "Blood Groups in Pakistan," *American Journal of Physical Anthropology*, 12, 3 (1954), 400–405.

thought. It was this group of specialists, the priests (Brahmans), who for the next 1,000 years were to shape Indian thought and give Indian civilization its characteristic qualities, seen as a series of paradoxes by the Westerner.

Hindu thought and belief center on the problem of individual salvation in a social context that is highly group-oriented. The means by which a person can seek salvation are varied: asceticism and withdrawal from society; the practice of the right social actions; devotion to deities; accumulation and distribution of property and goods; and the practice of physical sacrifice.

The quest of salvation through manifold means has caused Indian thought to be deeply concerned for more than 3,000 years with "the search for metaphysical truth, the nature of the cosmos, of god, of the human soul and the Absolute and man's relation to it." [4] The acceptance of manifold means toward salvation has led not only to an ethic of broad religious tolerance across the accepted avenues to salvation but also to rigid proscription of the means one's group has as its ordained path. There are elaborate rules as to how rituals are to be carried out and long and detailed discussions of the proper interpretation of a particular sacred text within a particular tradition of textual exposition. Underlying the great diversity in practice is the idea of duty (*dharma*), which is translated as law or religion, depending on the context. One must act in social as well as ethical ways. One's actions follow a pattern, and it is one's duty to follow the right action within the system of values one is committed to.

Structurally, Hinduism never developed a single orthodoxy that lasted for any period of time. There was no single source of either revealed or man-made truth, no church or church hierarchy. At various times, individuals, such as Sankarcharya in the ninth century, gained widespread acceptance of their particular interpretation of traditions and developed and accepted a set of rituals. But even when this kind of regulation appeared for a time, the rules and beliefs continued to change and diffuse, affecting groups in other parts of India in varying manner. There never has been, nor is there now, any one person or group of persons who can be turned to for binding authority on ritual, theological, or philosophical questions relating to all Hinduism and all Hindus.

Throughout the course of its history, Hinduism has displayed a constant dialectic between the thought and practices of the specialists and the religious activities of the masses. It is now almost impossible to say what grew from the religions of the peoples and what was created by

---

[4] W. N. Norman Brown, "The Content of Cultural Continuity in India," *Journal of Asian Studies*, 20, 4 (August, 1961), 431.

the specialists and diffused to the people. Anthropologists view magic as characteristic of folk religion, but one of the *Vedas* is concerned almost entirely with magic. W. N. Brown, the Sanskritist, found that at least half of the more than 2,000 folk tales and stories recorded by folklorists and others derived from stories embodied in the Sanskrit literature. It is now impossible to say what is a local oral tradition and what is derived from the refined literary tradition. The same is true of ritual practices. Blood sacrifice would seem to the anthropologist an aspect of local or village Hinduism, but animal sacrifice played a part in Vedic rituals.

Throughout its history, Hinduism has shown two opposed but complementary processes: absorption and compartmentalization. Time and time again, reform movements have developed within Hinduism; Buddhism, Jainism, the Bhakti cults, Sikhism, Lingayatism, the Brahmo and Arya Samajs, and the Neo-Buddhists are examples. Each of these religious movements started as a reform, often with social ends or expressing the social discontent of groups within Indian society. In some cases, as with Buddhism and Sikhism, they developed separate religions not considered to be part of Hinduism. Buddhism had all but died out in India proper, but in the last decade it has been adopted by Untouchables, primarily Mahars in Maharashtra and other parts of western India, as a means of cutting off the inhabitants from Hindu society and allowing them to better their social position. In 1951 there were 181,000 Buddhists counted in India, mostly in the eastern and central Himalayas. In 1961, out of a total of 3,256,000 Buddhists, almost 2,800,000 were found in Maharashtra and were the converted Mahars (or Untouchable caste). Whether this group will actually become practicing Buddhists and whether their conversion will help to improve their depressed social and economic status cannot be predicted at this time.[5]

In addition to Hinduism's taking form and developing during the period 600 B.C. to A.D. 600, political processes and structures that were characteristic of India until the eighteenth century began to take form. From the sixth to the third century B.C., the state system of India appears to have been made up of a number of regional and subregional entities, in some cases with a king (*Raja* or *Rajapati*); in other cases the states were "republican," in that there were no hereditary rulers but a corporate body that acted as a council. It was not until the fourth century B.C. that a widespread imperial system emerged under the Mauryas in

[5] Robert J. Miller, "Background to Buddhist Resurgence: India and Ceylon," in Robert Sakai (ed.), Studies on Asia 1966 (Lincoln, Nebraska: University of Nebraska Press, 1966), pp. 39–48. Eleanor Zelliot, "Background of Mahar Buddhist Conversion," Sakai, Ibid., 49–64.

northern India. The empire that exercised suzerainty over, or held as tributaries, all northern India also held some control south of the Vindhyas. The empire disintegrated after the death of Asoka in 232 B.C., and it was not for another 400 years that a widespread imperial system developed under the Guptas, who were based in present-day Bihar and expanded their rule to northern India but did not penetrate south of the Narbada River except for occasional military expeditions. The last major Hindu kingdom based in the north was that of Harsha of the seventh century A.D.

During the period between Asoka in the third century B.C. and Harsha in the sixth century A.D., peoples from central Asia continued to enter India, often establishing short-lived states in the Upper Ganges, the Punjab, or Rajputana. These peoples were soon absorbed into the Hindu social order. In southern India during this period, a pattern of regional states emerged: one in the Deccan Plateau; one on the Orrisan Coast; one on the southeastern coast; and one in the southern Deccan, in the area of present-day Mysore. These states must not be thought of in terms of modern nations with a total political and economic integration of all parts into a smoothly working administrative and political system. Rather, one must think of a multilevel state with varying kinds of authority and power vested at various levels: a local, a subregional, and a regional. The states frequently worked on an internal alliance system in which local chiefs or corporate bodies were partially incorporated through granting of legitimacy by a ruling family or group who centered their rule in their capital. Local rulers or groups were responsible for paying taxes raised from the soil-tillers and for providing troops to the central ruling power. In return they could be assured of their position as long as they did not challenge the central power. The ruler at each level was responsible for the maintenance of the social system; his legitimacy was expressed in the idea of the *danda,* literally the stick that symbolized his authority to use physical force to maintain the social system. This authority theoretically was exercised with the advice and consultation of the maintainers of the sacred traditions, the Brahmans; but in theory, though rarely in practice, the king could also create Brahmans, because he was the upholder of the caste system. The social and political systems were interlocked in terms of the relation of the Brahman to the Raja, with a sacred and a secular authority system coexisting, the sacred system being, in theory, superior, but with the Raja empowered to maintain and further the sacred authority.

In the eleventh century, large-scale incursions of the Islamic professing peoples began. These lasted until the eighteenth century. As we saw earlier, the invasion route to India was through the Khyber and other passes in the Hindu Khush. The first major invasion was led by Mahmud of Ghazni, who launched twelve raids for plunder and loot between 1000 and 1027. He raided as far as Saurathtra on the southeast coast, where his followers plundered the famous Somnath Temple, and as far as central Uttar Pradesh on the east. Mahmud's invasion was only the first of a continuing series, most of which followed a similar pattern: an Afghan, Persian, or central Asian population establishing a political base in Afghanistan, raiding the Punjab Plains to establish, after a time, a base at Delhi, then following the traditional invasion routes to the southeast and southwest.

The Islamic peoples from Afghanistan and central Asia had a social structure highly adapted to a raiding and military way of life. Most had a kinship system that put emphasis on the male lineage. Small groups of men traced their ancestry throughout an agnatic tie that often was reinforced with cousin marriage, creating, in a particular generation, strong ties among a small and tightly knit group of kin, but over generations separating relatives into small groups. Kinship rather than territoriality was the close tie among these Islamic peoples. From time to time, powerful leaders could organize these small kin groups into larger groupings for military purposes. In order to keep his groups together, the leader had to keep them moving and fighting.

These central Asian peoples had a technology geared to warfare and based on the horse and superb horsemanship. Cavalry tactics were the basis of their conquests of India. Even when they developed artillery, the horse was still their main offensive weapon.

Finally, they had in Islam an ideology to support their military and conquering proclivities. Hasan Nizami, chronicler of the activities of Muhammad of Ghuri in the thirteenth century, wrote, "He purged, by his sword, the land of Hind from the filth of infidelity and vice, and freed the whole of that country from the thorn of God-plurality and the impurity of idol worship, and by his royal vigor and intrepidity left not one temple standing." [6]

From the tenth century to the present, the relations between the two religions and their adherents sets one of the basic situations in the history, society, and culture of the subcontinent. In India and Pakistan today, there are approximately 150 million Muslims and 380 million Hindus. Most of the Muslims are not the direct descendants of the Muslim invaders but are converted Hindus, particularly from the earlier period of the Muslim invasions. Throughout the long period of interaction between Hindus and Muslims in the subcontinent, there have been periods of withdrawal and insularity at the cultural level and periods of rapprochement. At the folk level, given the large number of

[6] Quoted in Murray T. Titus, *Islam in India and Pakistan* (Calcutta, 1959), p. 12.

conversions in certain regions, there was little functional difference between Hindus and Muslims. It is at the theological-philosophical level that the differences between Hindus and Muslims seem greatest. To quote a recent student of the historical-cultural relations between Hindu and Muslim, Aziz Ahmad: "As a religio-cultural force, Islam is in most respects the 'very antithesis of Hinduism.'"[7] Hinduism, as we have seen, is a diffuse, individualistic religious system, putting stress, on the one hand, on concrete ritual acts of worship of the physical, symbolic representations of divine persons and forces and, on the other, on broad, speculative, and free thinking about eternal questions of right, morality, and the nature of the universe. Central to Islam, however, is the authority contained in a single work, the *Koran*, which embodies the divine word of God and the word of his Prophet. Speculative thought that has developed is secondary to the authority of the word of God and his Prophet. Islamic ritual is austere and eschews any representation of God, his Prophet, or human or animal forms for ritual purposes. Muslims, no matter what their home environment—Arab, Turkish, Persian, or Indic— are part of the *umma*, the Muslim community. At the theoretical level, the two religious systems and their view of the world and society are antithetical; at the functional level, the differences have become blurred.

The theory of Islam is easy to state, but the pristine simplicity, the unanimity in Islam at the time of the Prophet was long gone when the Islamic impact was felt in northern India. The Muslims were deeply divided into two antagonistic sects, the Sunni and the Shi'a, whose differences were partially geographical and partially theological. A strong mystical tradition, Sufism, had developed, finding fertile ground in India. In the seventeenth century, the Muslims in India were clearly differentiated among themselves on the basis of history and culture. There were the *Turanis*, the people who came from north of the Oxus River, from what is today part of the Soviet Union. These Turkish and central Asian peoples, principally the Mughals, began invading India at the beginning of the sixteenth century. There were the *Afghans* or *Pathans*, who had established the empire in northern India in the thirteenth and fourteenth centuries and who were strong in eastern India. There were the *Irani* peoples, who had migrated from Persia, although there was not a distinct Persian empire in India. It was the Iranis who most markedly influenced the Indo-Islamic culture developing by this time through their recruitment as civil servants, teachers, poets, writers, and doctors. Persian was the court language and the language of administration almost from the beginning of Muslim rule in India. Iranis rose high in governmental and military positions throughout much of the Islamic period in Indian

[7] Aziz Ahmad, *Studies in Islamic Culture in the Indian Environment* (Oxford, 1964), p. 73.

history. The fourth group, the *Hindustanis*, were numerically the largest category of Muslims in India. They were the descendants of Hindu converts or of invaders who had lost any identity with their original homes. Occasionally, Hindustani Muslims were able to establish regional states, such as the Rohillas of the eighteenth century in the territory east of Delhi, but usually they did not play a major political role.

In the eighteenth century, there were large concentrations of Muslims in two major areas: in the Punjab and in the mountains of the Hindu Khush, Sind, and Baluchistan; and in Bengal, particularly the eastern part. The distribution of Muslims in India today relates to significant earlier communities in Uttar Pradesh and Bihar, particularly in western and central Uttar Pradesh and in the area around Patna. There also were, and still are, scattered but significant communities in Gujarat and in the southern Deccan. These areas contained strong Muslim states in the eighteenth century. In addition, the Muslims tended to be urban populations; both the upper classes, who worked as administrators or had other connections with the government, and many of the urban artisans were Muslims.

In most of the environments where Hindus and Muslims found themselves during the Islamic period in India, there were varying degrees of interpenetration of cultures; in some respects, by the eighteenth century, a synthetic Indo-Islamic culture had developed. At the rural level, the synthetic or syncretic culture was represented by the use of ritual and social forms associated with the other religion by members of each religion. Most rural Muslims, many of whom were descended from Hindus, continued many of the same religious practices they had followed as Hindus. Many Hindus participated in Muslim sects and worship. For example, the cult of the *Pancho Pir,* prevalent in eastern Uttar Pradesh, was devoted to Muslim saints, and Hindus and Muslims alike went on pilgrimages to worship at the shrine of the five Pirs or saints. In manners, the Hindus of northern India, both of rural and urban elites, tended to follow Muslim dress, to use the courtly manners of the Persian Mughal courts, and to enjoy the music, art, and literature associated with the Muslim courts.

A number of Hindu groups, from long association with the Muslim rulers, particularly as civil servants, adopted many cultural forms from their employers. Among the most famous and important of these groups were the Kayasthas and the Kashmiri Brahmans. A portrait of Ganga Jhar, Jawaharlal Nehru's grandfather, shows him bearded and with a curved sword in his hand, in the style of the Mughal grandee.[8]

[8] B. R. Nanda, *The Nehrus: Motilal and Jawaharlal* (New York: John Day, 1963), p. 19.

CHAPTER SEVEN

The Mughal Period
and European Conquest

In 1498 three Portuguese ships under the command of Vasco da Gama dropped anchor off the coast of Malabar, climaxing fifty years of effort to find a sea route to the Indies. In retrospect, we know this event was a major turning point in the history of India and the history of the world, but the penetration of Europeans, their economy, and culture did not make a significant difference in southern Asia until the middle of the eighteenth century.

Two years earlier, in Soviet Turkistan, a sixteen-year-old Barlas Turk, Babur, began a successful career of raiding by sacking the great inland market of Samarkand. In 1519, Babur began to raid India and, in 1526, defeated the Afghans who were ruling northern India on the plains north of Delhi. In the following year, he defeated the Hindu Rajput chieftains southeast of Delhi, at Kanua, and established himself as the first of a line of rulers known as the Mughal Emperors. This Mughal dynasty lasted, technically, until 1858, when Bahadur Shah II was deposed by the British. Effective Mughal rule ended in 1748.

A view of the Mughal period and the Mughal decline in the eighteenth century is crucial to an understanding of the British conquest and the nature of British rule in India. In many respects, today's Indian society grows out of the conditions of the sixteenth to eighteenth centuries. When the anthropologist or the historian uses "traditional" Indian society as a timeless and spaceless referent, he is speaking usually of institutions whose roots are in this period. The basic pattern of Mughal rule was set by Akbar (1556–1605). As with any political system, Akbar had to develop a resource base to maintain his rule and establish personnel to ensure the maintenance of the resource base, to carry out policies determined by central authority, to maintain internal order, and to protect the interests of the state against internal and external threats. The resource base of the state was primarily agricultural. The problem faced by Akbar, as by his predecessors, was how to collect revenue from hundreds of thousands of villages containing the cultivators who actually produced both the crops to feed themselves and the surplus appropriated by others with a claim on part of the produce. There was a wide variety of claims on products of the soil. In the first instance, the tiller himself needed and had a right to a share of the crop. In most parts of India, the actual tiller had over him an individual family or lineage, claiming a substantial share of the crop. The rights of these superordinates and intermediaries between the tiller and the state had various origins: the clearing of virgin territory, often done by tillers under small groups of adventurers or the cadet lines of petty kings elsewhere, on the fringes of cultivated regions; conquest of a lineage of land controllers by another lineage; grant by some superordinate power of the right to dominate a small territory and to extract the surplus agricultural product from the tiller. Grants were also made not only to small military groups for political purposes but also to priests, learned men, and officials for services rendered.

The rights over the cultivator, then, were either by patrimony—which, following Eric Wolf, is the kind of domain exercised when control of the tillers and other occupants in the land is practiced by members of kinship groups—or by lineage and heredity. There can be several layers of patrimonial rights. The other major right over the tillers in Mughal India, called *prebendial,* was not vested in lineages or chiefs but was a grant of income allowed by the state to servants of the state or to individuals or groups, such as Brahmans, that the state wanted to support. Considerable lands, particularly in southern India, were in the form of prebendial domains to support temples and *maths* (monasteries). It was for the support of government officials, however, that most prebendial domains, especially under the Muslim rulers, were established.

Under the Muslims, holders of patrimonial domains were called *zamindars,* a word that, from the eighteenth century onward, came to be used by the British to cover any landlord, no matter what his origin. The lands of a zamindar were his *zamindari.* The holder of a prebendial domain for services to the state as a government official was called a *jagirdar* and his lands, his *jagir.* In addition, there were *khalisa* lands, lands directly controlled by the central government, that could be assigned as *jagirs* to office holders but that, when they were *khalisa,* were controlled by government officials. The third major kind of domain, far more common in Europe, was *mercantile* domain, in which the land was viewed primarily as private property of the landowner and as an entity to be bought and sold. This was uncommon in India before the end of the eighteenth century.[1]

The kinds of rights that landholders or land controllers held over their domains were by no means fixed. Holders of prebendial domains constantly tried to turn them into patrimonial domains, and patrimonial domains were taken away, usually through force of arms, and given to prebendial holders. In the patrimonial domains, a constant process of fission and fusion was at work in the land-controlling lineage. At a particular time, one person might control a large area, because inheritance, generally speaking, was equal among sons and there was no primogeniture except in royal houses. One generation's single landholder could, however, in three or four generations become a fairly large group of holders, who might hold their land corporately or divide it up. Individuals and small groups might move off to found new patrimonial domains with a single head or a single member.

The holders of the patrimonial domains tended to be from higher castes in society. In the north, in Bengal, they were Brahmans or Kayasthas; in Bihar, Muslims, often Afghans, Rajputs, Bhuminars (a caste that claimed status between that of Rajputs and Brahmans), and Brahmans; in Uttar Pradesh, Rajputs, Muslims, and Brahmans; in western Uttar Pradesh, Jats and Gujars; in the Punjab, Jats, Gujars, Rajputs, as well as some Muslims; and in Rajasthan and Madhya Pradesh, Rajputs, Brahmans, and a few Muslims. In the hilly areas, some tribal groups had the status of prebendial holders—the Raj Gonds, for example. Prebendial holders in Gujarat included Rajputs, Pattidars, and Muslims; in Maharashtra, Marathas and Brahmans; in the south, in Andhra, Kammas, Reddis, and Brahmans; in Tamilnad, Brahmans and high Sudra castes; in Mysore, Brahmans and Okkaligas; and in Malabar, Nairs and Brahmans. In the Dekkan parts of Mysore and Andhra were substantial Muslim holders. In the north, the dominant landholding lineages or important families did not usually live scattered in villages, as dominant castes do today, but were usually concentrated in a town-fort within the territory they controlled. On the land itself, in the villages, doing the tilling or supervising the tilling, could be representatives of these higher-

[1] For a discussion of the kinds of domains, see Eric Wolf, *Peasants* (Englewood Cliffs, N.J.: Prentice-Hall, 1966), pp. 50–54; for the kinds of landholders and landholding in Muslim India, see Satish Chandra, *Parties and Politics at the Mughal Court, 1707–1740* (Aligarh, 1959), pp. xv–1; and M. Athur Ali, *The Mughal Nobility under Aurangzeb* (Bombay, 1966). For southern India, see Burton Stein, "Coromandel Trade in Medieval India," in John Parker (ed.), *Merchants and Scholars* (Minneapolis, 1965), pp. 47–62.

caste land-controlling groups; but usually they were not of the same lineage or family as the land-controlling group. In villages might be cultivating castes, such as Lodhas, Noniyas, Mahishyas, and Kurmis, who did much of the actual tilling. They tended to have customary rights over land and could not be shifted about at will by the land-controlling lineage. In addition, providing much of the labor but without customary rights in land, were lower castes, such as Chamars, Namasudras, or Mahars. Both rural areas and town-forts housed craftsmen to produce needed tools, and others to provide services to both the tillers and the land controllers. Blacksmiths, carpenters, potters, weavers, barbers, washermen, water carriers, porters, and priests could be found in the countryside. Often specialized craft villages, in which a majority of the population was, for example, weavers or potters, produced craft products for use throughout the territory and for sale in urban markets. The town-fort may have had craftsmen as well who could produce luxury products for consumption by the land-controlling group and for sale to the outside.

The land controllers were also warriors, organized into quasi-military groups. They could be called on by their superordinates—whether officers of the royal power, which was superordinate to the land-controlling lineages, or the Raja himself, to fight with the royal army. In addition, military power was needed by the land controllers to protect them from outside groups who wanted to usurp their position. Also they frequently needed force, or the threat of force, to collect a share of the produce from the tiller. This share was divided into two parts: that used or sold for the land controller's own benefit, and that, usually in the form of money, transmitted as tax or tribute to the state.

In most parts of India by the seventeenth century, a system of allocation of the resources produced by the labor of cultivators could be thought of as consisting of three parts: that which went to the land controller for his own use, that actually redistributed to groups or individuals within his domain in exchange for products and labor, and that which was the state's share, used for maintaining central military forces. In the ruler's household, some was for consumption in the form of luxurious living and patronage of learning, art, literature, and the like, and some was used to maintain administration.

Akbar, like some of his predecessors, developed a system by which he tried to solve the three basic problems of resource collection, internal security, and the development of a functioning administrative system, with one solution. He tried to integrate and regularize the position of the zamindars, the property holders, by accepting the status quo and by trying to regularize the amount demanded from them through surveying their resources and setting an expected tax from them. The zamindars were to be supervised by a series of government officials who reached down at least to the town-fort level and who kept records for the state on how much was collected from what zamindars. These officials were sometimes paid directly, in the form of a salary, or with small prebendial grants in the local areas. They tended to become inheritors of their position, and their grants turned into small proprietary domains. Above these local official record keepers were other officials who tended not to be local and who could be shifted about. There was little specialization within Akbar's service, so that one year a man might be a revenue official in charge of a district, roughly comparable with an English county; in another year, he might serve at the court as an advisor or an official or in the field with the army as a military officer. The income for these officials came from their jagirs. Under Akbar, the location of an official's jagir and his posting were different. His jagir, as well as his posting, could frequently be changed.

The top officials under Akbar were of three origins: relatives and associates who had accompanied the Mughals into India; other foreigners who were Muslim, for, as Ali, a close student of the Mughal nobility, notes, "For the Persian, Chaghtai and Uzbek nobility, India had traditionally been an El Dorado where fortunes could be rapidly made"; [2] and a third group made up of zamindars and chiefs brought into the Mughal service as a means of integrating their territories into the Mughal Empire. Under Akbar, the higher nobility (slightly less than 500 of the top officials in the Empire) consisted of about 70 percent foreigners; of the remainder, about 20 percent were Hindu and 10 percent Hindustani Muslim. Under Akbar, most of these Hindus were Rajput chieftains from Rajasthan incorporated into the top officialdom as a matter of policy. To secure the allegiance of the chiefs of that area was crucial, because it lay immediately to the west of the Delhi-Agra region and was the route through which the subjugation of the west and the western coast had to be secured.

Under Akbar's successors, the Empire expanded southward across the Vindhyas, and the Mughals, for more than 100 years, were engaged in a series of wars and conquests, mainly against Muslim states established since the fourteenth century. These wars proved much more difficult than the conquest of the north, mainly because most of the terrain was hilly and because the Mughals were increasingly far from their main bases of manpower and supplies in the north.

It was the last of the major Mughals, Aurangzeb (1658–1707), who expended the most time and resources on the conquest of the south. At

[2] Athur Ali, *op. cit.*, p. 13.

the end of his reign, all but the very southernmost tip of the continent was under Mughal control, but this control rapidly disintegrated in the next 30 years. Under Aurangzeb, the upper official class expanded to 575, of whom 400 were Muslims and 175 Hindus. Later in his reign, the Marathas surpassed the numbers of Rajputs in the upper service, there being 73 Rajputs and 96 Marathas in the period 1679 to 1707. The Iranis and Turanis continued to dominate the Muslim part of the official class, with just half of the Muslims coming from these two categories.

Aurangzeb, like Akbar, used the granting of official positions as a means of winning over his enemies and incorporating them, their families, and their territories into his empire. In the early part of his reign, before he had made major inroads in the south, a little more than 10 percent of the upper official group were Dekkanis, people from the south, both Hindu and Muslim. By the end of his reign, about one-third of the upper officials were southerners.

The position and origin of the top official group, or nobility, as the historians call them, are less important than what happened to them. The nobility were the maintainers and diffusers of a new style and culture. This group, and some of those below them, may be thought of as a Persianized elite, because the culture of the Mughal court was basically Persian with admixtures of Turkish and Indian. A life style was established to which top groups of Muslims and Hindus could and did aspire. They were Urdu-speaking and Persian-writing, although they might also use their regional languages. They adopted Mughal dress with a shirt, a form of trousers, and the long Mughal coat. The national costume of Indian men today, the Sherwani and Pajama, in which Jawaharlal Nehru was most frequently seen, was a form of dress derived from the Mughal court. The pervasiveness of Mughal courtly influence on the culture of royal and zamindari India can be illustrated by the fact that when Shivaji, the Marathas military chief, who in the nineteenth and twentieth centuries has been viewed by nationalist historians as a "freedom fighter" against Muslim domination, was crowned, his throne rested on a tiger skin but had a canopy of velvet, a "grotesque combination of ancient Hindu asceticism and modern Mughal luxury." Sarkar, one of Shivaji's biographers, goes on to state that many of the symbols and trappings used at Shivaji's coronation were Mughal.[3]

The Mughal life style was felt by all who worked in the various states that succeeded the Mughals. Lucknow in the north, the capital of Oudh, and Hyderabad in the Dekkan, the capital of Hyderabad, continued into

[3] Judranath Sarkar, *Shivaji and His Times* (Calcutta, 1929), pp. 214–17.

the nineteenth century as centers of Mughal courtly culture. The Mughal style diffused down to the town-forts of the land controllers and among the many clerks and lower officials in the towns and cities, providing a model in content and form of a cosmopolitan culture for most of urban India and even for the countryside.

India, under the Mughals, experienced something of an economic expansion as well. With the establishment of a widespread empire, with a large capital, and the spread of subsidiary centers for regional and local government; the development and maintenance of a wide road network, uniform weights and measures, and a standardized currency; the reduction of internal trade barriers in the form of dues and customs within the empire, and attempts to make long-distance trade and travel safer—a market for both luxury and subsistence goods expanded, and some of the conditions were established under which this trade could be carried out. The Mughals and other participants in the luxury-consumption style established by them were particularly fond of fine textiles, fancy armor and weapons, and well-appointed palaces. At the time of this internal stimulus to trade and consumption, the Europeans were simultaneously beginning extensive commercial operations in southern Asia and using southern Asian goods in their trade with southeastern Asia and China.

The European mode of commercial operation was relatively simple. The Portuguese, Dutch, French, and British—the four major European groups involved in the Indian trade—all operated in much the same manner. Their companies were financed in Europe, whether with state money, as in the case of the French and Portuguese, or privately, as in the case of the Dutch and British. Ships were sent out annually, with bullion and some European trade goods, to stations or factories on the Indian coast. Initially these stations were established in or near existing ports and coastal commercial centers, such as Surat in Gujarat, Calicut in Malabar, Tranquebar and Pulicat on the Madras Coast, Masulipatam on the Andhra Coast, and up the Hughli River in Bengal. At these and other stations, the Europeans would leave a few men all year round to be responsible for the collection of the goods that the European trading companies wanted for both their Asian and European trade. There were three distinct but interrelated components that developed: Asian-European trade, inter-Asian trade, and country trade. In the early seventeenth century, spices, especially pepper, were the main products sought by Europeans for the European markets; from 1619 to 1621, 74 percent of the value of the Dutch trade from Asia to Europe was in pepper and other spices. This had fallen to 27 percent by 1700, replaced in importance by textiles, which accounted for 16 percent in the earlier period and rose to 55 percent by 1700.[4] Spices and pepper came mainly from the islands of southeastern Asia and Malaya, although India, particularly Malabar, produced some pepper. To obtain the pepper and spices, Europeans had to deal in Indian textiles, the principal item of interest to the producers or controllers of spices and pepper in southeastern Asia. So the inter-Asian trade was based, in the seventeenth century, on European trade goods and bullion traded on the Indian market in exchange for textiles, which were then shipped to southeastern Asia for spices and pepper, which in turn were shipped to Europe. In addition, Europeans became involved in the country trade within India, in bulk agricultural commodities like rice and textiles.

The Europeans had little actual contact with Indian producers in order to obtain the goods they sought but were dependent on Indian middlemen, who were brokers and, in some cases, employees of the companies. In the sixteenth and seventeenth centuries, trade in India was closely tied to politics. Political appointments at the major ports and markets were looked on by Mughal officials as being very lucrative. In southern India, in particular, the state tried to maintain monopolies in goods traded and shipped. Many large trading efforts began with state initiative. In order to carry on their trading activities, European companies had to maintain good relations with the rulers in whose territory they were based and were trying to operate. This was done by attempting to obtain legal permission or licenses to trade. Frequently Europeans would be equipped with such licenses from the Mughal emperors, but found that they would not be honored by local or regional officials and that various forms of bribery were necessary to enable them to carry on their activities. In turn, the Portuguese, Dutch, British, and French had control of the seas around India and in southeastern Asia, because European naval technology proved superior to Indian and Arab naval forces. At particular times, Europeans would use this naval superiority to further their trading goals; but, by and large, until the middle of the eighteenth century Europeans did not intervene in a substantial military manner in the political system of India. The territory that Europeans, with the exception of the Portuguese, controlled was granted by the Indian powers and not based on conquest.

From the beginning of the fifteenth century until the middle of the eighteenth century, European activity—with the exception of the Portuguese, who in the fifteenth century did a considerable amount of proselytizing and established land bases and local governments, particularly on the west coast of India—was limited to commercial activity and the

---

[4] Kristif Glamann, *Dutch Asiatic Trade 1620–1740* (The Hague, 1958), p. 13.

sporadic application of military force to protect their local trading interests. Europeans did affect the nature of overseas trade. They stimulated the textile production of India and began to attract to their settlements commercial and artisan groups whose future was tied to Europeans.

In a relatively short time (1739 to 1763), the pattern of European activity and goals that had been characteristic for 250 years changed radically. The change initially grew out of the competition between the British and French for political and commercial dominance in southern India. This competition was an extension of their rivalry in Europe. At the same time, the political system of India was reverting to the pattern of regional states without the strong central power that had characterized India under the Mughals. The British and French began to use their troops, Indian and European, on behalf of local rulers of the southern Indian states in their wars against each other. An alliance system developed in which the British had one set of allies and the French another. The alliances were based on the provision of troops by the companies to their allies, in return for which the Europeans got exclusive trade rights or direct payments in the form of land assignments. European troops or European-trained and led troops proved superior to indigenous troops organized along traditional lines. This was partially a question of tactics: the British developed infantry tactics to counter Mughal-style cavalry tactics. Closely tied to the question of tactics were the recruitment and discipline of the Indian troops by the British. Although British troops tended to be organized in regional caste units, they were essentially recruited in small groups whose loyalty was to their unit rather than to their own chief or leader, in contrast to indigenous troops, who were organized along kin and caste lines or around a leader who had other than military ties to them.

Most Indian battles in the eighteenth century were won or lost by subversion of leaders rather than by direct military confrontations. The British ultimately achieved military superiority because of their ability to make their Indian as well as their European-raised troops loyal to their units and their calling as military men rather than to the particularistic values of kin, caste, and locality. This was done by regular payment of wages, direct control by European officers of relatively small-scale units, and the fact that their forces tended to win, thus providing a tradition of victory and plunder that was useful in developing unit loyalty.

In the struggle between the British and the French in the middle of the eighteenth century, control of the seas around India became crucial. With control of the seas, land forces could be shifted about, supplies, men, and money from Europe could be obtained, and trade could continue to help finance military ventures on land. After initial setbacks,

British sea power proved to be superior. Initially, the French had an advantage in the leadership of Dupliex and Bussy, who proved more sophisticated in their capabilities with Indian allies and in using Indian states and troops for their own tactical and strategic ends, but with the loss of sea control, the French moved their center of power inland and their trade suffered accordingly. British financial resources proved more flexible, and the British East India Company and Parliament were willing to support the Indian venture.

The British victory at the Battle of Plassey, in Bengal, in 1757, when the British, under Robert Clive, defeated the army of the Nawab of Bengal and his French allies, is taken symbolically as the establishment of the British Empire in India. For the next sixty years, until 1818, the British continued a series of wars against the Indian states on a piecemeal basis and, bit by bit, brought the subcontinent under their military, administrative, and diplomatic control. With the final defeat of the Marathas after intermittent warfare for forty years, the British controlled India. Although they continued through the nineteenth century to carry out military operations, particularly in the northwestern frontier, the effective conquest of India was completed by 1818. Territory continued to come under direct, as distinct from indirect, British rule until 1858.

CHAPTER EIGHT

Cultural and Structural History: Nineteenth and Twentieth Centuries

In the period 1760 to 1790, the British in India had to find means by which they could control the territories and the people who had become their subjects. In the middle of the twentieth century, it is hard to realize how quickly and with what little experience the British devised a system of colonial rule. In a few years, the British in India changed from being a trading company—whose officials were mainly devoted to keeping commercial accounts, inspecting trade goods, and directing and negotiating with their Indian brokers and employees regarding trade matters—to having to rule 40 million subjects in the Andhra Coast—the Norther Circars, acquired in 1766—Bengal, Bihar, and Orissa, for which they took administrative responsibility in 1765. Throughout British rule in India, natives of Britain never accounted for more than 0.25 percent of the vast population of the subcontinent.

The central questions continually faced by the British in India were how to develop a political-military system they could use, leaving much of the actual day-to-day functioning of the government in Indian hands, and how to devise successful means of supervising the activities of these Indian subordinates.

The first problem the British faced was the collection of revenue. They needed a secure financial base to support their armed forces, their own administrative costs, and the costs of their commercial activities. The British started with the principles of assessment and collection of revenue that the Mughals had developed in northern India. The first British effort was to find individuals who would be responsible for the payment of the land revenue, assessed on the basis of what previously, under Indian rule, had been collected from local areas. The responsibility for payment of revenue rested on a whole series of individuals and groups whose rights were variously based. Some revenue payers based their rights on conquest or on clearing the land, others on royal grant; others were tax farmers who had rented from the government the right to pay the revenue for the difference between what they collected from tillers and intermediaries and what they were obligated to pay to the state.

The first major decision, which became one of the bases of British revenue policy, was made in Bengal in 1793 when approximately 3,000 individuals of widely diverse rights and varied origins were by law made the *zamindars* (landlords) of Bengal. The British, only partially comprehending the significance of their decision, treated these *zamindars* as if the legal rights they established were like those of English landlords, including the right to sell, mortgage, and transmit through inheritance the titles to their lands. The sole responsibility of the *zamindars* was prompt and full payment of the revenue demanded by the government; failure on the part of a landlord to pay led to the sale of his lands to another landlord who claimed he could pay the revenue. The legal change involved was considerable, because it completely ignored the previous relationships among tiller, intermediaries of various kinds, and the state.

Until the coming of the British and the establishment of their rule in India, control of land was much less significant than control of people who worked on the land. In pre-British times, the land controller was a controller of people. Land, of course, was crucial to the social order: one needed land to support followers who, in turn, were needed to protect one's interests against other land controllers and the state. As discussed above, the pre-British military system was partially based on the need of the state to use the followers of local land controllers for its own army and of the local land controllers to have enough power to collect their share of the produce from the tillers. The British developed a military system directly under their control, recruited, trained, organized, and paid for by (and for) the state. They could therefore eliminate all organized local military power within the domains of the local land controllers. Although local land controllers still maintained "strong-arm men," either members of their lineages or employees, they could be used only within their own lands and did not pose a threat to British domination. In every area the British brought under control, they forced the disbandment of local military forces and systematically destroyed the forts and fortified houses of local land controllers. Unlike their predecessors, the British monopolized all legitimate use of force; and although, in actual functioning, landlords continued to use direct force to maintain their revenues and keep internal foes and the tillers in subjugation, this exercise was extra- or at best quasi-legal. With land becoming an entity that could be bought, sold, and frequently sold for arrears of revenue and, with the tie between local military forces and land control broken, a new set of relations between the person or group designated as the landlord and the state, on the one hand, and between the tillers and new kinds of intermediaries, on the other, began to develop.

Another factor that began to affect the rural social structure under the British was the expansion of agricultural production for sale in markets. In some respects Indian agriculture has always had a commercial component. India has supported cities and craft production, courts and luxury consumption, as well as a range of service functions, both rural and urban, all requiring food and raw materials derived from agriculture. In pre-British times, grain had to be supplied to cities and towns for both the military and the government. A wide range of other agricultural products, such as sugar, tobacco, and spices, were sold widely. Cotton and jute products were needed for weaving, indigo and other agricultural products for dye stuffs. Under the British, the commercial component in Indian agriculture increased markedly by the end of the nineteenth century. Some of the increase was in plantation agriculture, such as tea and coffee production. The direction of plantations was in the hands of British owners; the profits went to British firms. Cotton in western India was grown for export to supply British mills. Grains, such as wheat grown in the Punjab, were exported to Europe and distributed to Indian markets. Rice production rose in the Delta regions of the south, and sugar became an increasingly important product in northern India during the nineteenth century.

Economic historians continue to debate the effects of this commercialization of India's agriculture and the question of who derived benefit from the expansion of agriculture in the nineteenth century. Some claim that all the benefit and profit went to the British, who were exploiting the Indian agriculturalists. In fact, some argue that changes in the agrarian structure devastated the countryside, leaving the tiller prey to small groups of rapacious landlords who drained everything from the land. It has also been argued that Britain was using India primarily as a market for British manufactured goods, mostly cotton textiles manufactured in England, and that the British destroyed the widespread craft industries of the countryside. This destruction caused the rise of landless laborers, resulting in a large pool of cheap labor that eventually depressed the income of all the agriculturalists.

The question of what happened to the agrarian structure of India, both in terms of its social and its economic organization, has just begun to be studied empirically, with the quantification necessary to an under-standing of what happened, distinct from what people thought had happened. No single set of generalizations can cover the complex changes that took place. It is more than likely that in different regions there were different patterns of change, depending on the nature of land control, the local ability to increase land under cultivation, the nature of the tax structure that the British established in different regions, and the regional potential for the development of cash crops. The nature of the rural social structure under the British has been further obscured by the British administrators' involvement with the legal structure of landholding and their constant attempts to regularize or change relations that were centered on land by law and administrative regulation. His-torians have tended to follow the British records, focusing on questions of changing policy and law in the study of the land structure of nine-teenth- and twentieth-century India and assuming that the legal cate-gories, such as *zamindar* (landlord), *pattidar* (co-sharer in a corporate body that stands as the landlord), and *ryot* (peasant proprietor), defined groups or strata in the rural society. Similarly, in legal categorization of various tenants, it has been assumed that the origin of the tenant made significant sociological differences.

In the latter part of the nineteenth century, there was also great con-cern about the social origins of those who obtained the legal rights as landlords. Everywhere except in southern India, it was assumed that there were ancient aristocrats who, by royal ancestry or long-term status, traditionally had been overlords of the soil. There were also traditional cultivators and other groups, such as merchants, writing castes, and Brahmans, who, although they may have been part of the rural social order, did not have landlord or cultivating rights. Much legislation, par-ticularly in the Punjab and in Bombay, was concerned with the "pro-tection" of the ancient aristocracy and the cultivators.

Stated in sociological terms, the legal categories of landlord and tenant and the kinds of landlords or the assumed origins, ancient or parvenue, are less important than an understanding of the local pattern of political control and dominance and the actual distribution of control of the product of the soil. In most parts of India, including the south, where there was supposed to be small-scale peasant proprietorship (*ryowari* ownership), much the same pattern in distribution of the legal rights of land ownership was characteristic of the late nineteenth century in India. At one end of the scale in the distribution of legal rights was a small group of landlords having the legal rights over a third to a half of the lands and, at the other, a very large group of land-lords holding rights over the rest of the land.

For example, in Madras Presidency in 1892, 804 landlords "owned" 38 percent of the land, but only slightly less than 3 million others had landlord rights over about 61 percent of the land.[1] What does the distribution of land rights in this situation actually mean? How different are the social structures of villages that are part of large estates held by one holder and those in which there are many holders? Are the villages of small holders richer or poorer? Are villages where there is one landlord, usually living in a town, more egalitarian? Is there a different pattern of political structure at the village level in the two situations? We do not know the answers to these questions.

It has been assumed, but not demonstrated quantitatively, that there are marked differences between villages dominated by powerful landholders and villages made up of small peasant proprietors. From the studies of anthropologists during the 1940s and 1950s, it seems that there is not necessarily any significant difference in social, political, and economic structure in the two situations if one takes the perspective of the village and the villager rather than that of the city and town, or the large-scale landlord and the administrator and politician. In the late nineteenth century, as in the middle of the twentieth, the understanding of the social, political, and economic structure of rural society was based, not on a distribution of legal rights, but on a whole series of other variables: the size of the village, the number and kinds of castes found in it, the relation to transportation and marketing facilities, the crop pattern, the presence or absence of large-scale craft production, and the ecological niche occupied by the village. These variables seem to affect the structure of villages more than whether the landlord rights are vested in one person or many.

Who were the powerful landlords, where did they live, how did they control their lands and the people on them, and what was their style of life? These landlords tended to be urban-dwelling, and although they maintained a house, or houses, within their estates, they tended not to be present within their areas. They collected their share of the income from the land in various ways. In Bengal, as well as in some other regions, a system of intermediary landlords grew up. The revenue demanded by the state in Bengal, Bihar, Orissa, and eastern Uttar Pradesh was fixed in perpetuity by the British. In these areas, those who held the position of tiller or supervisor of tillers often had their rents fixed, not by law but, by custom. Various other limits were set on the amount that cultivators had to pay to those with the legal status of landlord. In return for a fixed annual payment, the landlords often sold to others

[1] B. H. Baden-Powell, *Land Systems of British India,* 3 (Oxford, 1892), 142.

the right to collect the rents, either for a period of time, or absolutely and in perpetuity. They were thus freed from any responsibility, effort, or expense in the collection of the rent and the payment of the revenue to the state. In turn, these intermediaries often sold all or part of their rights. In other instances, landlords employed agents to collect rents and to forward the rents to their headquarters.

In most areas where there were large-estate landlords, no matter whether they collected their share of the income through agents or through formal or informal sale or lease of their landlord rights, the crucial questions were who had actual control and dominance over the tillers, and how was the income from agriculture divided. Some British officials, many urban-based Indian nationalist leaders, and historians, often visualize a situation where one landlord, and perhaps his relatives and employees, lord it over a multitude of depressed, spiritless, rent-racked "peasants," all of whom are at a severe level of poverty and powerlessness in the local social and political system. There were un-doubtedly some places where this was the situation; however, in many or most places, it was not. Very often, no matter what their legal status, rural groups were the actual controllers of the tillers. In some places they were the descendants of the previous land-controlling lineages. Although their legal rights may have been sold off, as they frequently were in the nineteenth century, they still controlled the tillers and retained considerable land, at fixed rates as permanent tenants. Often these former holders were in a very good position, because of their numbers and their control over the tillers and others in the village, to fend off and often immobilize the powerful landholder, who faced the choice of a continuous sub rosa kind of warfare in the villages, or coming to some kind of compromise with the established controllers of the tillers of the soil. It was this latter course that seems most often to have occurred.

In most of India and through much of the nineteenth century, both agricultural production and prices paid for agricultural produce rose; the amount of income derived from agriculture therefore increased. Although in some parts of India the revenue structure was adjusted every ten years to account for the rise in prices, and in much of India the pitch of the revenue demand was generally high—frequently as much as 50 percent of the value of the assumed production—nonetheless, there seems to have been relative prosperity in much of rural India until the last decades of the nineteenth century, when the agricultural popula-tion increased to the point where available land was fully occupied.

In the large *zamindari* areas there were two or more levels of land and cultivator control: the level of the large *zamindars* who were ab-sentee landlords, a level of their employees or subholders, and a level in which there were large permanent tenants or small landlords who had effective control over others in the rural social structure. In every part of India from the late nineteenth century and until the present, it is the substantial peasant, the man who may have had 20 to 100 acres under his control, who was and is the key figure in the social structure rather than the very big *zamindar* or "royal" personage with *zamindar*-like rights over a territory or domain.

Frequently, through kinship and marriage, these substantial peasants were linked in lineages or segments of caste groups, and their kin and caste mates lived in surrounding villages. They were often in a state of enmity toward their fellows and competed for economic and social status with them. But they could unite in opposition to the landlord and his agents and could continue to dominate those lower than they in the caste hierarchy. Professor M. N. Srinivas has called such groups dominant castes.[2] Dominant castes are castes within local areas that control much of the land, have fairly large numbers, and are relatively high in the caste hierarchy. In the twentieth century, their rural dominance has been buttressed frequently by their connection to local administrators and to local political leaders and through taking advantage of new educational opportunities leading to urban incomes, part of which flows back into the rural areas.

These castes exercised and continue to exercise their dominance in a number of ways. They control others in the villages through structured systems of dominance, such as the *jajmani* system, in which land and its products are redistributed in return for services, both ritual and non-ritual. But it is the land and the land controller who are at the center of the redistribution. The dominant castes frequently have direct control, through monopoly, of access to land for cultivation and building. The relations between the land controller and the actual land user are not only contractual but often involve leader and follower relations in local political matters. The dominant castes can use their control of land to bind others to them as followers. Frequently, the land controllers, or dominant caste, provide credit both in cash and in seed grain for food to others in the village. The land controllers frequently exercise judicial functions in settlement of local disputes among those below them in the village. Their dominance, in the final analysis, is based on and can be exercised through their application of violence in the form of beatings, crop cuttings, and physical dispossession of land and houses. Given their better access to the local police and local officials, the dominant caste can usually be assured of relative immunity from legal sanctions on the part of local officials.

[2] M. N. Srinivas, "The Dominant Caste in Rampura," *American Anthropologist*, 61 (February, 1959), 1–16.

Almost half of the land area of pre-Partition India was known as the Princely States, not administered directly by the British Crown in India but nominally the domains of princes and chiefs. The 562 Princely States, which covered 45 percent of the land, included 24 percent of the population. The states varied greatly in their size and importance. The largest was Hyderabad, and other important ones were Jammu and Kashmir, Mysore, Gwalior, and the larger states of Rajputana. Much of central India, Gujarat, and highland Orissa was divided into many small states. There were some differences in agrarian structure among the Princely States, as in British India. There were many Royal Estates in the larger Princely States, and there was a tendency within the Princely States to continue to use land as prebendial domains in order to reward service to the state and to pay salaries. There was also usually a connection between the land controllers and the royalty, with a tendency for kin and caste fellows of the royal family to be land controllers. In effect, the pattern in the Princely States was an extreme form of the pattern found in British India.

Since the beginning of the nineteenth century, when Charles Metcalf, a British official attached to the Mughal Court in Delhi, described Indians as living in "Village Communities" which "are little Republics, having nearly everything they want within themselves, and almost independent of any foreign relations," [3] a well-developed picture of the nature of the Indian village has spread widely. In this view, the village was economically self-sufficient, producing the goods and services it needed and consuming what it produced. There was division of labor among the cultivator, the artisan, and village servants based on shares of the agricultural product. There were few, if any, landless laborers.[4] The village, with a council (*panchayat*) made up of the elders of the village directing its social and political life, was assumed to be self-governing and self-regulating. This view of the idyllic premodern Indian village is a myth. No systematic evidence has been brought forward to support these assumptions about the village, and most who hold this view of the Indian village continue to quote and refer to the same few reports by early British officials, such as Metcalf, and a few travelers.[5] Three in-

[3] Originally written in 1830 and quoted by Percival Spear, *Twilight of the Mughals: Studies in Late Mughal Delhi* (Cambridge, 1951), p. 117.

[4] See Surendra J. Patel, *Agricultural Labourers in Modern India and Pakistan* (Bombay, 1952), pp. 32–34.

[5] For a discussion of the myth, see M. N. Srinivas and Arvind Shah, "The Myth of the Self-sufficiency of the Indian Village," *Economic Weekly*, 12 (1960), 1375–78; Louis Dumont, "The Village Community from Munro to Maine," *Contributions to Indian Sociology*, 9 (1966), 67–89; and Dharma Kumar's careful study of agricultural labor in southern India in the nineteenth century, *Land and Caste in South India* (Cambridge, 1965).

tellectual-cultural strands have gone into the myth and its perpetuation. The first is the romantic and evolutionary myth of some of the British officials, who, early in the nineteenth century, saw India as they wished to see their own past—gentry surrounded by happy peasants. Grafted onto this, in the middle of the nineteenth century, were notions about the evolution of society from communal property-holding groups to private ownership; since India was backward, it clearly must have had this older form of property-holding organization and society. The second strand is Marxist, which again emphasizes the organic unity of the interrelationships of hand weaving and hand tilling. Marx believed that British imperialism would inevitably destroy this kind of society and economy and that the destruction was a necessary stage in the development of Indian society.[6] The third strand in the development and maintenance of the myth is contributed by Indian nationalists. They saw pre-British India more or less idyllically, with happy peasants and craftsmen in their villages, with no strife, no poverty, no domination by landlords, and on the verge of industrial development based on the craft industries. It was British imperialism and its goal of exploitation of the Indian masses that account for the poverty and landlord domination of the rural social structure we see in the twentieth century.

The only way we can learn something about the structure of Indian villages in the early nineteenth century is to study actual villages on the basis of surviving revenue and other records. There are extant only a few detailed, published accounts of particular villages at this time. The most complete is that by Thomas Coats, an East India Company surgeon who collected material on the village of Lony, outside of Poona. His description of the village was based on work done in 1819, two years after the area came under British control. Table 8 is an enumeration of the population according to occupation, in July, 1819.

Most obvious is the heavy dependence on agriculture for livelihood in the village, with 81 percent of the population directly dependent on it (hereditary cultivators, 39 percent; cultivators on lease, 29 percent; Mahars, who acted as agricultural laborers, 8 percent; hired servants and slaves, who were also agricultural laborers, 5 percent). There were eighty-four families of cultivators (all of the Kunbi caste) of which 50 had either proprietary or customary shares of the land. The Kunbis were clearly the dominant caste in the village in terms of numbers, landholding, and the fact that the village *Patels* (headmen) were Kunbis.

Thirty-five families, all of whom were owner-cultivators, were of one lineage, that of the headmen. They claimed to be descendants of

[6] For Marx on India, see Daniel Thorner, "Marx on India and the Asiatic Mode of Production," *Contributions to Indian Sociology*, 9 (1966), 33–66.

TABLE 8

The population of Lony, July 1819

Occupational group	No. of families	Males	Females	Children	Total	Percentage of population
Hereditary cultivators	50	55	73	89	217	39
Cultivators on lease	34	54	56	52	162	29
Brahmans, priest and accountant	3	6	5	10	21	4
Carpenter	1	1	1	2	4	1
Washerman	1	1	2	. . .	3	1
Barber	1	1	2	. . .	3	1
Potter	1	1	1	4	6	1
Silversmith	1	1	1	2	4	1
Dresser of idols	1	1	1	2	4	1
Water carrier	1	1	1	2	4	1
Shoemaker	2	3	3	. . .	6	1
Watchman (Mahar)	13	16	16	16	48	8
Mohammedan sacrificer	1	1	1	3	3	1
Jain shopkeeper	3	4	8	9	21	4
Marwari shop-keeper	2	2	. . .	. . .	2	. . .
Police servants	3	4	3	4	11	2
Mohammedans	4	4	6	7	17	3
Hired servants	. . .	11	. . .	. . .	11	2
Slaves	8	8	7	3	18	3
Total	130	175	187	203	565	—

SOURCE: Thomas Coats, "Account of the Present State of the Township of Lony," *Transactions of the Literary Society of Bombay* (London, 1823, reprinted 1877), p. 194. Paper read February 29, 1820.

the original land settlers. Those Kunbis who cultivated on lease did so on the lands of the proprietary Kunbis. They appear to have been highly mobile and "when they find that they can subsist elsewhere they quit the village." [7] Most of the Mahars and all the hired servants and the male slaves were landless agricultural workers; approximately 30 adult males were exclusively landless workers. In the 1950s, G. S. Ghurye and his students did a restudy of Lony and found that the population

[7] Thomas Coates, "Account of the Present State of the Township of Lony," *Transactions of the Literary Society of Bombay* (London, 1823, reprinted 1877), p. 242.

had more than doubled—to 1,400 persons, of whom only 45 were landless workers.[8]

In terms of occupational structure, ten of the caste households in the village counted by Coats were hereditary servants of the village (*Balatadors*); these were the carpenter, washerman, barber, potter, silversmith, dresser of the idols, water carrier, shoemaker, and Mohammedan sacrificer. In addition, there were two other hereditary servants, an ironsmith and a ropemaker, who were not residents of the village. These servants provided necessary goods and services in return for the use of land and fixed annual payments in grain from the cultivating households. The three Brahman households provided priestly service, and one of the households also supplied the keeper of records of the village. There were five households of merchants, three Jain from the Karanatic and two Marwari.

One interesting aspect of the description of Lony, in relation to the idea of the self-sufficient village, is the degree of cash indebtedness in the village; 68 of the 84 families of cultivators were in debt for Rs. 14,532, or about Rs. 211 per indebted household. The debts were held locally by shopkeepers or Brahmans.[9] The debts were incurred, according to Coats, to pay for weddings, purchase cattle, or buy food. In addition to cash debts, about a quarter of the inhabitants were in debt to their neighbors for grain or fodder. Land sales were also "not infrequent." [10] The village had a school with classes in reading, writing, and arithmetic that was attended by children from the headmen families, the Brahmans, and the shopkeepers. Coats was surprised, however, that many of the villagers had a considerable knowledge of the leading events and history of their own country and he thought they were better informed than the lower classes of Great Britain. Coats also noted that the villagers were very fond of traveling to temples in the area at the times of annual fairs, where, after making their offerings and receiving *prasad* (sanctified food), "They saunter about the crowd, converse with acquaintances that come their way, listen to story tellers, look at jugglers and tumblers, and finally purchase what they may be in want of together with sweetmeats and toys for such of their family or friends as have remained at home." [11]

Unlike many of the villages of upper India that were dominated by lineages or clans spread over a number of villages or were part of little kingdoms, Lony seems to have been politically self-contained. The *Patel* or village headmen held office directly under a government grant (*wa-*

[8] G. S. Ghurye, *After a Century and a Quarter* (Bombay, 1960), p. 14.
[9] *Ibid.*, p. 226.
[10] *Ibid.*, p. 242.
[11] *Ibid.*, pp. 219–20.

tan), which defined the duties, rank, ceremonies, and perquisites of the holders. The duties of the headmen were to collect the government revenue, encourage people to settle in the village (a considerable amount of the village in the early nineteenth century appears to have been cultivable waste), punish minor crimes, and settle disputes among the villagers. There was also a *kalkarni* or record keeper, who was a hereditary government servant as well; he kept measurement of the fields, lists of holders and their rights, and a list of all the inhabitants and their dues to the government.

The picture we derive of one Maharashtrian village in the early nineteenth century, at the advent of British rule, shows a high degree of monitization, involvement, at least in the surrounding region, some mobility on the part of the nonpermanent cultivators, fairly specialized governmental functions of headmanship and record keeping under the government, land sales, a considerable amount of indebtedness and commerce, with five shops for a village of 500, and no craft production other than for agricultural tools, shoes and leather goods, and pottery for domestic consumption.

Unfortunately, we do not have in published form any similarly detailed descriptions of other villages from this time period. There are, however, some occupational statistics for selected districts at roughly the same time. In Bihar District, in Bihar, Francis Buchanan collected statistics from local officials and other knowledgeable men in the area. At the beginning of the nineteenth century, Buchanan broke down the population into four categories: gentry, who comprised 26 percent of the households; plowmen, 63 percent; artificers (craftsmen), 8 percent; and traders, 3 percent of the population.[12] W. H. Sykes, statistical Recorder of the Bombay Presidency in the 1820s, estimated that, for the northern part of Maharashtra, at least "three quarters of the population are directly engaged in agriculture."[13] In the District of South Konkan, on the basis of a census taken by Pelley in 1821, approximately 150,000 of the adult males in the population of 202,000 were found to be directly engaged in agriculture, and about 12,000 in craft activities, such as blacksmithing, saddle making, tailoring, weaving, stone cutting, basket making, and copper- and goldsmithing.[14]

---

[12] Montgomery Martin, *The History, Antiquities, Topography and Statistics of Eastern India* (London, 1838), Appendix of Statistical Tables, p. 1.

[13] W. H. Sykes, "Special Report on the Statistics of the Four Collectorates of the Dukhun, under the British Government," *Report of the Seventh Meeting of the British Association for the Advancement of Science*, VI (1837), 266.

[14] Calculations based on tables in Durgaprasad and Bibhavati Bhattacharya, "Report on the Population Estimates of India, 1820–30," *Census of India, 1961*, pp. 161–64.

India in the early nineteenth century, as today, had a significant urban component. It is, at this time, however, impossible to make any reasonable estimates concerning the distribution of rural and urban populations in early nineteenth-century India. The first problem relates to the size of the Indian population before 1872, when the first census of all India was completed. The census of 1872 found a total of 203 million persons in India; subsequently, demographers and officials of the Census of India have demonstrated that this estimate was too low and that at this time the population was more probably in the range of 250 million.[15]

The earliest attempts at estimating the population in India in the nineteenth century were those of Walter Hamilton in his work, *Geographical Statistical and Historical Description of Hindustan and the Adjacent Countries,* vol. I, which was published in 1820. Hamilton's estimate of a population of 134 million was based on a close study of East India Company records and the few published accounts of particular parts of India that were then available. Robert Montgomery Martin estimated the Indian population in 1838 to be 200 million.[16]

Martin, later quoting an official East India Company estimate, put the population of India in 1855 at 172 million.[17] Both Martin, in 1855, and Hamilton, in 1820, gave lists of cities in India with population estimates. Hamilton listed 27 cities with a total population of 4,250,000, or 3.2 percent urban, and Martin listed 42 cities with a population of 5,100,000, or 3 percent urban. Neither of these lists is in any sense complete for even the important cities, let alone all other population centers that could be considered, which were, in some sense, urban.

Europeans consistently underestimated the rural population of India in the first half of the nineteenth century. Rural habitations were and are scattered over the countryside; estimates based on land records consistently underrated the actual number of people, because British estimators were mainly concerned with landholders. Early observers greatly overestimated the populations of the larger cities. Indian cities constantly struck the European observer as very crowded and congested, because the streets were narrow, with buildings right up to the

---

[15] For a discussion of the population estimates and census, see Kingsley Davis, *The Population of India and Pakistan* (Princeton, N.J.: Princeton University Press, 1951), chap. 4 and appendix A.

[16] Robert Montgomery Martin, *Statistics of the Colonies of the British Empire* (London: W. H. Allen, 1839), p. 294.

[17] Robert Montgomery Martin, *The British Colonies* (London: London Printing and Publishing, 1850), p. 502.

edge of the street; markets and pilgrimage places always seemed thronged and swarming with people. Banaras was thought to be India's most populous city in 1820 by Hamilton, who gave a figure of 600,000 for its population. His estimate was based on Lord Valentia's estimate published in 1809, in turn based on an estimate by the Indian *Kotwal* (Chief of Police), who clearly inflated his count to impress his employers with the magnitude and difficulties of his office. James Prinsep, British Mint Master in Banaras in the 1820s and an early Sanskrit scholar, conducted two counts of the population of Banaras in the mid-1820s; one, based on a register of houses kept for tax purposes, came up with an estimate of 181,000 persons, with roughly another 22,000 in the suburbs, or a little over 200,000 altogether. He also carried out a count by caste and occupation based on first-hand investigation and the estimates of the heads of various castes and trades. This count came to 155,000. Prinsep thought it should include an added 26,000 for children not estimated and for visitors and unavoidable omissions, bringing the count to approximately 180,000.[18] With an underestimation of the urban population and no accurate statistics for either urban or rural, it is impossible to state what the size of India's urban population was in the early nineteenth century.

In 1881, the census estimated that 9.3 percent of the population in India was "urban"—that is, living in places of 5,000 inhabitants or more. It is reasonable to think that the situation in the early nineteenth century was not much different from that at the end of the century. Industrialization was barely beginning, although there had been increases in the major cities through the nineteenth century with the centralization of various administrative and commercial functions in the port cities and the provincial capitals. A very crude estimate, then, for urban population in the early nineteenth century would be 6 to 9 percent. In 1961, 18 percent, or more than 70 million persons, were counted as urban.

The number of people counted as urban in the early or the late nineteenth century is much less important than the nature and consequences of urban living in India at that time. India, of course, has a long tradition of urban ways of life. In India, however, as in other pre-industrial societies, living in a city and following an urban way of life mean something different from living in a highly industrialized economy and society. In the late eighteenth and early nineteenth centuries, cities performed four major functions: economic, as a center for marketing, trade, commerce, and craft production; military, frequently as military centers, with forts or walled areas for defense purposes; political, as centers of political

[18] James Prinsep, "Census of the Population of the City of Benares," *Asiatic Researches*, 17 (1832), 470–98.

life where chiefs and rulers or their officials had their courts; and finally, religious, sometimes as sacred centers containing concentrations of ritual specialists, scholars, and devotees. No matter what the origin of the city historically, most of these functions were found together, although one or another of them might dominate at any particular time. Most of the major northern Indian cities and many of those in southern India owed their origin to political considerations, that is, the location of the regional chiefs or rulers in the city. This can be seen clearly in the shifts that occurred during the eighteenth century. In the seventeenth century, Dacca in East Bengal was the leading city in Bengal; it was the provincial capital and had at least 50,000 military and civil personnel connected with the government.[19] This number of people alone would account for the city's growth when one thinks of the services required in terms of food supplies, building, entertainment, clothing, and equipment. Typically in the history of Indian cities, a ruler wanted to put his physical stamp on the city by constructing imposing and beautiful buildings for public, domestic, and ritual use. In Dacca the great builder was Shaista Khan. In addition to its administrative functions, Dacca was the center of a considerable textile industry that drew European merchants. Both the court and the Europeans stimulated the development of the textile industry that, in turn, affected general trade patterns, making Dacca a center for internal as well as overseas trade and creating a need for banking and other services.

In the beginning of the eighteenth century, the capital of Bengal was shifted by Murshid Quili Khan from Dacca to Murshidabad on the Hughli River north of Calcutta. There was an important textile and trade center nearby, at Kasimbazar. With this political shift to Murshidabad, Dacca, although it remained an important commercial center, lost its preeminence as a city to Murshidabad. In turn, by the middle of the eighteenth century, again accompanying a political shift, Calcutta, the British capital of the Bengal Presidency, supplanted Murshidabad. In 1822, Calcutta had 180,000 people, and it was estimated that another 100,000 entered from and returned to the nearby suburbs and villages every day.[20]

By the beginning of the nineteenth century, the three European-founded ports—Calcutta, Bombay, and Madras—were becoming the major cities of India, a distinction they continue to share, particularly for commercial and industrial functions. European interests in general, and British interests in particular, were initially responsible for the develop-

[19] Abdul Karim, *Dacca: The Mughal Capital,* The Asiatic Society of Pakistan Publications, 15 (Dacca, 1964), 29.

[20] Bhattacharya, *op. cit.,* p. 234.

ment of these cities. Efforts were made in the late seventeenth and early eighteenth centuries to attract Indian craftsmen into the cities. In Calcutta, there was already a village of weavers; in Madras, there was also interest in having weavers and other textile workers settle in the city. In Bombay, which developed early as a shipbuilding center, great efforts were made to attract Parsi builders from Gujarat. Throughout the eighteenth century, the port cities tended to be settled on a caste basis, and, like other Indian cities, much of the local government was actually in the hands of caste-based groups living in their own quarters, *mohallas*. Characteristic of the port cities, and soon to be characteristic of those up-country cities with any major governmental functions, was the difference between the Indian and the European parts of the city. Up-country, the European quarter usually was on the outskirts of the city, where government offices, courts, and frequently the military cantonment were often established. Europeans built large, low, open houses with pyramidal roofs—bungalows, a word we still use, which is derived from *bangala* or "from (or of) Bengal."

Indians in the new cities initially continued to build the kinds of houses that had been characteristic of urban architecture in the north under the Muslims. They were substantial houses of two, three, or sometimes even five or six stories of masonry, with a few windows and an unadorned facade, built right up to the lane or next to the street. Inside the house was usually an inner courtyard or a walled courtyard, with a small garden where much of the life of the household took place. If the family consisted of shopkeepers or traders, the front part of the house was also used for commercial purposes. Later, in the nineteenth century, Indians inside the city began to adapt the European-style bungalow to their own use, frequently making it several stories larger. The bulk of the Indian population lived in mud and thatched houses in and around the city. Often a large house of a substantial family, well kept and with elaborate gardens, would be close to squalid quarters for servants and "hangers on."

Something of the internal structure of cities in the early nineteenth century can be learned from Table 9. The data in the tables must be interpreted with great caution because of the way in which the census was taken. In three of the four cities—Banaras, Bareilly, and Anusphahr—the census categories of occupation were based mainly on caste. Only in Dacca did the observers systematically try to obtain actual occupations from within the broad categories of caste. The least reliable data are those in the categories attempting to separate actual cultivators, landlords, or agricultural laborers from the general category of "service," which was used in all four censuses as a catchall phrase. Service in-

TABLE 9

Occupational Structure of Four Indian Cities 1820–30 *

(Number percentages have been rounded)

	Banaras 1827	Bareilly 1822	Anupshahr 1830	Dacca 1830
Population	180,000	66,000	8,000	67,000
Households	30,400	13,160	1,710	16,255
Religion Hindu	144,000 (80)	40,000 (60)	6,200 (78)	31,500 (47)
Muslim	36,000 (20)	26,000 (40)	1,800 (22)	35,500 (53)
OCCUPATIONS				
Landholders Public Service	26,000 (17.4)[1]	2,500 (19.0)[2]	270[2] (15.7)[2]	2,962[2] (19.0)[2]
Cultivators and Laborers—Medium castes	25,200 (16.4)	2,600 (19.8)	100 (5.8)	3,343 (20.7)
Cultivators and Laborers—Low caste	3,000 (2.0)	400 (3.0)	200 (11.7)	189 (1.2)
Weavers etc.	12,100 (7.9)	1,220 (9.3)	130 (7.5)	748 (4.6)
Carpenters/Blacksmiths	4,000 (2.6)	320 (2.6)	50 (2.9)	243 (1.5)
Craft—other	8,000 (5.2)	1,050 (8.1)	45 (2.7)	770 (4.8)
Trading and Banking	11,300 (7.4)	750 (5.8)	310 (18.0)	761 (4.7)
Food Processing Retail sale of food	13,600 (8.8)	1,180 (8.9)	90 (5.4)	3,459 (21.4)
Personal service Barbers, washermen, servants	9,200 (6.0)	1,300 (9.9)	120 (7.2)	297 (1.8)
Ritual specialists	22,000 (14.3)	500 (3.8)	140 (8.2)	130 (0.8)
Scribes, clerks, teachers	9,500 (6.2)	900 (6.8)	100 (5.9)	76 (0.5)
Transportation	2,500 (1.8)	80 (0.6)	60 (3.5)	105 (0.7)
Entertainers	3,800 (2.5)	260 (2.0)	30 (1.7)	357 (2.2)
Other	2,700 (1.8)	100 (0.8)	65 (3.6)	2,815 (17.1)
	153,700 +26,300 (child)	13,160	1,710	16,255

1 Figures based on individuals.
2 Figures based on households.

SOURCES:
Banares: James Prinsep, "Census of the City of Benares," *Asiatic Researches*, XVII (1832), 470–98.
Bareilly: Robert Thomas John Glyn, "Enumeration of the various classes of population and of trades and handicrafts in the town of Bareilly in Rohilkhand, formerly the capital of the Rohilla government," *Transactions of the Royal Asiatic Society of Great Britain and Ireland*, I (1827), 467–84.
Anupshahr: "The Town and Neighboring Country of Anupsheger," in Durgaprasad and Bhabhavati Bhattacharya (eds.), Report on the Population Estimates of India (1820–1830), *Census of India* (1961), pp. 283–84.
Dacca: Bhattacharya, *Op. Cit.*, pp. 285–327.

cluded people who worked for the government as clerks and lower officials, were employed by landlords as agents, were hangers-on of large
households, or were employees of commercial houses and assistants in
shops. On the basis of the materials, it is impossible to sort the category
"service" into reasonable groupings. The large category "other" is, in
Dacca, a reflection of the better quality of the census, because it included
a large group of households whose occupation was listed only as "house-
holders." These may have been households in which there was no obvious
means of support and, from the little data given on household composition, it might be inferred that these were households of elderly people.
There was also great difficulty in grouping the various occupations and
castes. In Banaras, more than 200 separate castes and occupations were
listed, and almost 200 for Bareilly and Dacca. In each case, the names
and occupations listed in the separate censuses were often different, so
that some guesswork went into the development of the categories and
the assigning of the specific caste and occupation to each of the major
categories.

Even with unreliability of data and analysis built into the tables, some
ideas about urban social structure can be gained. The distinctive character of each of the cities can be seen. Banaras, the great shrine city
of India whose major activity was as a ritual center, contained a large
number of ritual specialists, 14.3 percent of the total. Anusphahr in the
present Bulandshar District of western Uttar Pradesh on the Ganges
was, in the late eighteenth and early nineteenth centuries, an important
commercial center for trade in indigo, a vegetable dye much in demand
in Europe. Because it was located at a crucial crossing of the Ganges,
it was also an important bathing place for regional pilgrimages. Its
commercial and ritual significance is reflected in the fact that 18 percent
of the households were engaged in trade and banking, and 8.2 percent
were ritual specialists. Both Banaras and Anusphahr were essentially
Hindu cities; the important local Raja was Hindu. In western Uttar
Pradesh, in the late eighteenth century, Bareilly was an important
regional capital of a Muslim dynasty, the Rohillas, that controlled a good
deal of territory immediately east of Delhi. This is reflected in the relatively high percentage of Muslims in the city, 40 percent in a region
in which no more than 15 percent of the population were Muslim.

Bareilly had just begun to decline as a royal center, but the presence
of royal power could be seen in the large number of craftsmen and those
engaged in personal service. Dacca, which had flourished in the late
seventeenth and much of the eighteenth centuries as a textile and
marketing center, had begun to decline sharply in significance by 1830.
Henry Walters, who was responsible for taking the Dacca census, esti-

mated that the population there had declined by 50 percent in a sixteen-year period.[21] Walters attributed the drop to the East India Company's decreasing investment in cloth and other manufactured goods, starting as early as 1801. Of the three cities, Dacca had the fewest craftsmen, with Bareilly having three times as many craftsmen as Dacca, and Banaras having twice as many.

Overall, though, a pattern of a very large number of upper caste persons—Brahmans, Rajputs, Kayasthas, and Muslims—living off agricultural lands or government and private income does emerge. With the exception of Anupshahr, the number of identifiable untouchables was low. In each case, there were also specialized agriculturalists, such as Mali and Koeris, living within the cities and apparently engaged in market gardening. The city included much agricultural land, generally on the outskirts, but one can speculate that there were open areas that were farmed, even in more populated parts of the cities, as in the case of smaller towns and cities today.

There were several life styles in the cities of the early nineteenth century: cosmopolitan, local, and regional. Banaras, in some senses, was at the same time the most traditional and the most cosmopolitan of Indian cities. There was a strong Maharashtrian group in the city, many of whom were self-imposed exiles from Maharashtra after the breakup of the Mahratta confederacy, coming with their fortunes and pensions to live out their lives in Banaras. Many of the temples that mark the river front of Banaras today were financed by Mahratta princes and their Brahman preceptors. There were 3,000 Bengali Brahmans in Banaras in 1827, many of them scholars and priests, others working as clerks and officials of the British. The Muslim community of Banaras was split between a large number of weavers and landed groups. Muslim weavers, Julahas, were the largest single community in the city; most lived in close proximity in a few *mohallas.* The other large Muslim groups were deposed or exiled members of the royal families from Delhi and Lucknow, many of whom still had considerable income and property elsewhere. Frequently, important landlords from all over India maintained houses or palaces in Banaras and spent part of their time in religious activities in the city. In Banaras traditional Brahmanical life styles existed simultaneously with cosmopolitan Persianized life styles of the Delhi court and the local cultures of eastern Uttar Pradesh and western Bihar.

21 *Ibid.,* p. 326.

CHAPTER NINE

Urbanization, Education, and Social and Cultural Change

Changes in urban social structure and life styles in India did not develop in the cities, such as Banaras, Bareilly, and Dacca, which in terms of the size of their population remained static or declined during the nineteenth century and diminished in importance as cultural, intellectual, and commercial centers compared with the great port cities of Calcutta, Madras, and Bombay. Banaras, which had a population of 180,000 in 1827, had increased to only 223,000 by 1891, to 266,000 by 1941 and to 489,600 in 1961. Calcutta, however, grew from around 200,000 in 1820 to 744,000 in 1891, 2,108,000 in 1941, and 2,927,289 in 1961. Madras, which was thought to have between 200,000 and 300,000 people at the beginning of the nineteenth century, grew, from 425,000 people in 1891, to 800,000 in 1941, to 1,729,000 in 1961.

Population growth of the port cities, particularly Calcutta and Bombay, was based on the beginning of large-scale industrialization in the middle of the nineteenth century in the cities and surrounding areas. Cotton textiles in Bombay and jute manufacturing in Calcutta were important industries by the middle of the nineteenth century. In both cities, port facilities and attendant functions also grew rapidly during the nineteenth century. Madras, Calcutta, and Bombay developed into major educational centers with the establishment of the university system in 1857. Governmental functions also increased, with Calcutta as the capital of the Presidency of Bengal as well as of British India. Madras and Bombay were also presidency capitals. The administrative functions of the cities provided large numbers of jobs for lower officials as well as for lawyers, agents, and others concerned in their private capacity with government action. The port cities were the headquarters of a wide range of British firms engaged in industrial management, banking, and commerce, all employing large numbers of Indian subordinates.

The structural changes implied in the development of the port cities, in the nineteenth and early twentieth centuries, and of the transportation, commercial, and industrial centers, were not felt until later in the nineteenth century. But by the third and fourth decades of the nineteenth century, the process of cultural change that historians and sociologists subsume under the concept "Westernization" had begun for small but significant groups in the cities. Authors use the terms "Westernization" and "modernization" carelessly, sometimes interchangeably, to cover all kinds of changes experienced by the Indian population in the nineteenth and twentieth centuries. I use the term "Westernization" to cover broad-scale cultural changes—values, ideas, and life style—modernization in the nature of social relations, stratification, and basic economic structure. It is clear that modernization in the sense of structural change and Westernization in the sense of cultural change are linked and fused processes. People's thoughts about what they are doing, and their justifications for it, may be as important as changes in structure in understanding change in India. Above all, it should be kept in mind that it is Indians we are talking about when we discuss change. The origin of a steel mill, historically, may clearly be an aspect of Western technology, and the changes it will bring in the life style and social relations of those who work in it are examples of modernization and Westernization. But to the Indians, the origin is less important than their own creative cultural and social adaptations to the situation. Little has been borrowed: few of the cultural and structural changes that have taken place in India are not distinctively Indian, no matter what their source. Modern technology and ideas can be utilized by a traditional culture, and traditional ideas can be of great use in a modern culture.

The introduction of printing and modern communication media affords an illustration of the complexities of modernization and Westernization and their relationship to what might be termed the redefinition of traditional culture. Printing in Indian languages was introduced largely by Western missionaries who wanted to make the Bible and Christian tracts widely available as part of their efforts to convert the Indian people to Christianity. In the early nineteenth century, the East India Company's government also encouraged printing and publishing to facilitate administration. As seen earlier, Indian vernaculars and literatures were highly localized and often limited to particular groups, so that, before publishing materials in the Indian languages, efforts had to be made to standardize the languages. In addition, once Indians became printers, individuals and organizations began to publish for their own interest and not for the interest of the state or the Western missionaries.

There was little control over what could be published, particularly over religious literature and creative writing. Although literacy was low in India in the nineteenth century, still there was, in absolute numbers, a large reading public that took to reading published works, whose distribution was, of course, many times wider than that of manuscript books and pamphlets. Many of the materials published in the nineteenth as well as the twentieth century related to traditional culture and values. Texts, stories, fables, accounts of rituals, religious guides, and lives of religious figures were and are published in huge quantities in India. People who never before had access to the ideas and ideals of Hinduism now do. The major religious reform movement of the nineteenth and early twentieth centuries in northern India—the Arya Samaj—was closely tied to education and printing in Hindi. In the twentieth century, education and, consequently, literacy have greatly expanded in India; lower-caste groups have now become literate. Westerners tend to think that education is a way of modernizing a society, and in some respects it is if the content of the education and what people read after they have become literate are based on assumed Western values of achievement, individualism, rationality, and empiricism. Certainly many college-educated Indians are exposed in a variety of ways to Western thought. But it is an open question whether those who have received a primary school education that equips them with literacy in the standard language of their region are similarly exposed to Western values.

In Senapur, a village where I did field work in 1952, some of the Chamars, the Untouchables, were literate and did read. But they read versions of sacred stories that stressed traditional values. One Chamar in particular, a young school teacher, was well versed in the traditions of Hinduism, all of which he had learned from reading. Traditionally, Chamars have been prevented from learning, in any formal way, about the tenets and practices of Hinduism. Brahman priests do not serve them. Under Vedic law, Chamars are supposed to be mutilated if they hear the Vedas, and they were barred from entry into temples. In the last 100 years, a religious movement called the Siva Narayan sect, which has a few temples in major cities, such as Bombay and Kanpur, became very popular among the Chamars. In many villages, Chamars have a *mahant* (leader) of the sect who holds regular prayer meetings and rituals at which the sayings of the founder of the sect are read. The trappings and symbols used are traditionally Hindu. Many of the leaders and some of the members of the sect owe their identification and participation in the sect to urban experience. In the cities, Chamars have attended the temples of the sect and have been exposed to teachers and proselytizers for the sect. In a very real sense, literacy and urban experience, supposedly sources of change toward modern and Western structures and values, have become for the Chamars a source of values and behaviors which were, to this point, denied them and which are traditionally Hindu in content. The institutions, technology, and skills that we think of as leading to Westernization and modernization can often lead to traditionalization.

For some groups in Calcutta, Bombay, and smaller cities, though, there were, by the middle of the nineteenth century, the beginnings of cultural change. Individuals such as Ram Mohan Roy, Dedendranath Tagore, Henry Derozio, Iswarchandra Vidyasagar, and others of the educated and English-using community of the Bengalis, for example, began to try to incorporate Western religious ideas and modes of thought into their understanding of their own culture. They were often obsessed with the direct criticism of the British officials and missionaries of some practices associated with Hinduism and they wished to change some of their own customs, such as early marriage for girls and the burning of widows on their husband's funeral pyre.

It is difficult to summarize the ideas of these early Bengali writers and thinkers in the first half of the nineteenth century and to isolate precisely what was new, what general, and what idiosyncratic. Through much of their writing, however, several themes constantly recur. The basic theme for these new intellectuals was that they were living in a new era and a new dawn was breaking; they felt that they were living in a renaissance.

Central to the new ideology and culture these men were trying to create was the goal of purifying Hindu thought and culture. They wanted a Hinduism, based on the Vedas and the Upanishads, which stressed thought and belief, not practice, and which eschewed worship and ritual at temples and the use of images. Many of these practices were criticized by Europeans as idolatrous. The Bengali thinkers sought to integrate Western ideas, rationality, monotheism, and individuality with their religious views. The search to reconcile the ambivalence inherent in their adaptation of Western thought led to the idea that the "new intellectuals" were between two cultures. Individually they sought to resolve the tension they believed to exist between Western and Indian thought.

Another major theme was the rediscovery of the past of India, in which Indians had once lived in a golden age after which degradation had set in. This golden age turned out to be like Western culture of the nineteenth century, with rationality, monotheism, simple democratic customs, equality of men and women, and a level of technology higher than that characteristic of mid-nineteenth-century India. The fourth major theme was that there could be a conscious and self-directed reform of the society and culture of India. I think the idea that individuals could analyze their own customs and religion and then consciously set about changing them, with social ends in mind, was an innovation in Indian culture. The great reformers of the past—the Buddha, Sankachariya, the Bhakti poets—were largely concerned with man's relation to the supernatural. They had essentially otherworld concerns, and the social consequences of their ideas were almost by-products.

Later in the nineteenth century, other themes began to emerge in the ideology of Western-influenced elites in the cities: ambivalence toward and, finally, rejection of the British. Early writers and thinkers, such as Ram Mohan Roy, and even later cultural nationalists like Bankim Chandra Chatterjee saw and deemed worthy of emulation great virtures in individual Britishers and in British culture and society: honesty, integrity, courage, and physical strength. As British attitudes of racial superiority became more pronounced in the latter nineteenth century and as official policies were increasingly framed to the disadvantage of the Western-influenced elites, an increasing dislike of the British as colonial exploiters and a more positive view of Indians themselves became characteristic of the new ideology. Coupled with the cultural nationalism emerging from the search for roots in their own past was the tendency of Indians to become more provincial in their views. Identification with regional traditions, gods, and heroes began to replace the more abstract glorifications of Hindu thought and the Hindu past.

In recent years, historians have tried to connect the cultural and intellectual changes that developed, particularly in Calcutta, with structural changes in Bengali society. Thus far, no single line of analysis has proved adequate to understanding the developments in Calcutta from the middle of the eighteenth century until the beginning of the twentieth century. The families of the Western-influenced elites, although within Bengali upper-caste society, were diverse in origin. How they made their money varied, how they maintained their social and economic positions varied, and, to a large extent, even their styles of life varied. A few things can be said of their origins, though, which seem to hold for a large number of the important Bengali families of the period.

No matter what their place in pre-British Bengali society, those families who became important in the early and middle nineteenth century show a connection with the British in the form of an ancestor who served as a *banyan* (broker) for the Company, or for an individual Englishman, or for someone who served as a judicial or revenue official. Income derived and, more important, information from any connection with the British could then be turned into successful commercial or land-acquiring activities. The secret of economic success in the late eighteenth and early nineteenth centuries appears to have been the ability to diversify one's activities among landholding, private commercial, and proto-industrial activities, government-connected commerce, such as military contracting, and the liberal professions, particularly law and teaching.

Early access to and use of new educational opportunities also seem to be crucial in this group of families who became important in Calcutta life. The Hindu College, founded in 1817 as a joint effort by some British officials and wealthy Bengalis, provided an education in English for most of the important families, who realized that success could be achieved through a knowledge of the English language. The founding and main- tenance of the Hindu College brings one again to the paradox of reversal and intertwining of "modern" and "traditional," both characteristic of social change in India.

It is conventional in the picture of early nineteenth-century India to oppose two figures viewed symbolically as the extremes regarding mod- ernization in that era: Ram Mohan Roy, the great modernizer, who wanted to direct Hindu and Indian culture toward a Western model, and Radha Kant Deb, who is looked on as the defender and upholder of the status quo and traditional society. Yet it was Radha Kant Deb and his father, who played a key role among the Indians, who founded the Hindu College, which was based on the financial help of many of the leading landlords and Rajas of Bengal rather than on the urban-based "new wealth." The Debs have been regarded by historians as the archreac- tionaries in Calcutta society, the upholders and defenders of Hinduism in its traditional form against Ram Mohan Roy and his followers in the Brahmo Samaj. The difficulty in examining the relationship and antago- nisms between the advocates of a new Hinduism and Indian society and the traditional defenders lies in the fact that both the Debs and Ram Mohan Roy participated, in a sense, in a new intellectual environment in which voluntary associations, petitions, public meetings, published tracts, newspapers, and periodicals were the battleground of dispute. In the dispute, the real traditionalists—the pandits, the illiterate and semiliterate masses—were not even aware of what was happening. Much of the argument was among a small number of the citizens, and the terms of discourse for both "modernists" and "traditionalists" were new.

In the long run, it may have been the educational institutions—par- ticularly the Hindu College, the Calcutta School Book Society, and the Calcutta School Society—that did more to shape the new culture of Calcutta than did the more spectacular religious reform societies like the Brahmo Samaj. The committees and societies needed to support and run the new educational institutions were a structural departure in the society. In the Calcutta School Book Society, Hindus and Muslims, landlords and merchants, government employees and pandits joined in a common cause bound by a mutual social goal rather than by ties of territory, kinship, or allegiance to a patron, as was characteristic of older forms of organization in India. The notion of the voluntary association was widely accepted by the middle of the nineteenth century. There were landholders' associations, associations for social reform, such as the Poona Sarvajnik Sabha, and by the end of the nineteenth century, literary and scholarly associations. These groups were small in membership, some were ephemeral, but there was increasing experience on the part of the Western-influenced people in Indian society with organizational activity that was in contrast to traditional kinds of groupings and that had different aims.

POLITICAL CHANGE

The single most important structural change that took place in Indian society between the end of the eighteenth century and the present relates to the political system and the institutions and attitudes connected with it. The British in India monopolized the legitimate use of force. As we have seen, previous government rule was partially based on the utilization of local and regional military power to further the ends of the central government. No previous government had the technological and bureaucratic skills necessary to develop a military system, with legitimate force at their disposal, that could ignore others in the society. This monopolization of legitimate force at the governmental level would not have been possible if the legitimacy of British rule had not been largely granted by elites within the society. British rule, like previous Mughal rule, was legitimate by the right of conquest in the eyes of significant groups in the society. To the majority of the population in the nineteenth century also, British rule was legitimate, since they were the *raj*, the ruler. That the granting of legitimacy by the Indian population was not always total can be seen by the widespread revolt that started with the Bengal Army in 1857. In large parts of Uttar Pradesh, western Bihar, and some parts of central India, significant numbers of the population joined with army troops to overthrow British rule, rallying around the symbols of dispossessed eighteenth-century rulers: the Mughal Emperor in Delhi; the last of the Peshwas (the Maratha rulers), Nana Sahib; the Rani of Jhansi; and local rulers, such as the dispossessed Talukdars of Oudh. Later in the nineteenth century, there were other much smaller-scale movements of this kind in which local people bound by primordial ties of locality, kinship, or religion revolted against the authority and legitimacy of the British government.

In the late nineteenth century, members of the small Western-influenced urban elites gradually began to argue for a larger share in the management of the British state in India. Their arguments were borrowed in part from European nationalist movements and based on ideas of the right of self-determination; they were based in part on a claim to equality of jobs access in the administration of the state, because many of the Western-educated Indians had ability equal to that of British civil servants. The movement was also based in part on a heightened sense of the educated Indian's understanding of his culture and his past. Increasingly this small elite group gained organizational experience, in voluntary associations, in local self-government at the district level, through advisory capacities at the policy-making level of the provinces, and on appointed or selected councils.

The first generation of Indian nationalists, such as Surendranath Banerjee, Ferozshah Mehta, and G. K. Gokhale, argued for more self-rule following the ground rules established by the British Raj within the authoritarian bureaucratic structure of government. The early nationalists debated and reasoned with their rulers. They believed in the reality of British values: reason, the effectiveness of marshaling information, and argument to achieve political ends. The British were receptive, though more so at home in Parliament than in the office of the British rulers in India, and gradually began to expand the franchise and to elevate the responsibilities of councils.

The early nationalists began their campaigns at a time when economic, educational, and social changes that had their beginnings in the middle of the nineteenth century were taking root. The number of English-educated was infinitesimal compared with the population of India, but the number of graduates of Indian universities and colleges grew with each decade. The opening of the elite British-manned Indian Civil Service to Indians in the 1860s turned out to be a source of great frustration. Few Indians were able to qualify for appointment, although they had the prerequisites, because the entry to the service was manipulated by the British rulers to the disadvantage of the Indian applicants. Indians with good degrees from Oxford, Cambridge, and the University of London found themselves unable to achieve the higher academic ranks in Indian universities, because the chairs in many subjects were reserved for Britishers. Experienced and well-trained assistant magistrates and collectors, no matter what their credentials and knowledge, had to defer to much less experienced and more junior British officials in the management of the districts, for the youngest and newest British recruit to the Indian Civil Service in effect outranked any member of the lower civil services, composed of Indians.

The building of a large railway network in the second half of the nineteenth century was the basic factor in the integration of the Indian economy and its incorporation into world markets. The well-being of the Indian peasant became increasingly tied to world markets in wheat, jute, cotton, and rice, as Indian agriculture, which always had a commercial component, became increasingly commercialized, not only in plantation crops of tea and coffee, but also in crops grown by the substantial peasantry.

Modern large-scale industrialization in cotton textiles and jute milling, as well as smaller-scale industry related to the railways, grain, and sugar mills, and the provision of some consumer goods within India developed largely through European capital and managerial ability, with little attempt to incorporate the Indian business communities into the modern industrial economy. Banking became almost a preserve of the British. Some Indian financiers in Bombay and Ahmedabad were successful in the textile industry, but even they felt forced to rely, in the nineteenth century, on British technological and managerial skills.

Throughout the last decades of the nineteenth century and the beginning of the twentieth, the perception grew of the gap between the capabilities that members of the educated Indian elite felt they had and the role they were allowed by the British rulers in the economy and political life of their own country. In the beginning of the twentieth century, the nationalist elite itself became split in ideology, goals, and views on how the goals could be achieved. The older leadership felt that the more rationalist and gradual approach through acquiring more and more self-rule from the British would be successful, because they still granted to the British government the legitimate right to rule India and still accepted the British evaluation of the Indians as not ready for rapid entry into self-government. Other younger leaders began to advocate more radical approaches to self-rule. They wanted to involve a broader spectrum of the Indian people in the movement, and they approached the masses by using traditional Hindu symbols and heroes and summoning a more vigorous Hindu reaction against foreign rule. Terrorist groups devoted to acts of revolutionary violence began to form in Bengal and Bombay. This terrorism was met by repressive measures on the part of the British government, which, in turn, heightened the prestige among Indians of those jailed for revolutionary activities. The call for a wider incorporation of the Hindu population into the nationalist movement and the frequent use of Hindu nationalist symbols in the revolutionary activities had the effect of alienating large numbers of Muslims who felt they would be disadvantaged in a Hindu state.

Increasingly, the British looked on both the moderates and the radicals as part of a conspiracy rather than as the expression of legitimate Indian strivings for self-government and independence. The British constantly pointed out that the leaders of the nationalist movement and most of its participants represented only a small fraction of the society and were only furthering their own self-interest. The British justified their rule by attempting to picture themselves as the true protectors of the Indian people, the peasants. Meanwhile, the British strengthened their ties to the powerful landlords and the princes who, they argued, were the natural leaders of the Indian people—a people accustomed to despotic rule. The British, with the development of a wider franchise, tried to make the constituencies communal; that is, Muslims, in effect, would vote for Muslim candidates, Hindus for Hindu candidates. The rationale was that it would protect the rights of minorities; the effect, intended or not, was to heighten the difference between communities and afford the opportunity to increase animosity between groups in the society. In 1905 there was a burst of political activity on the part of Indians, particularly the Bengalis, over the partition of the province of Bengal, which the British government maintained was too large. The area consisted of the provinces of Bengal, Bihar, Orissa, and Assam. But instead of separating the non-Bengali-speaking areas and leaving East and West Bengal as a unit, the British split the Bengali population between two newly created states, one predominantly Hindu and the other Muslim. The articulate and effective Bengali leaders saw this as furthering the British policy of "divide and rule" and punishing their opposition to British rule. There were widespread disturbances, mass meetings, and acts of terrorism. In addition, the Bengalis attempted a boycott of British goods for the first time and called for the establishment of their own educational system and for the production of the goods they needed themselves.

Bengal was reunited in 1911, by which time the imperial capital had been shifted from Calcutta to the newly built New Delhi. The agitation over Bengal was important because it confirmed in some of the leaders their belief that only through direct action would they achieve self-rule and eventual independence and that they needed social and economic philosophy and plans as well as the political goal of self-rule. The differences in ideology and methods that grew out of the partition of Bengal led to a split in the Indian National Congress, the organization that had provided the overall forum for Indian nationalism. With the coming of the First World War in 1914, the movement quieted down, because the British government in India sought the cooperation of the nationalists and implied that, with the successful completion of the war, many of the nationalists' demands would be met.

In 1914 Mohandas Gandhi, a Gujarti English-trained lawyer who had gone, in the early twentieth century, to South Africa after a brief attempt to establish a law practice in India, returned to India. In South Africa, Gandhi found that his countrymen who had migrated there as laborers and shopkeepers lived under severe legal and social disabilities. It was there that Gandhi first used his methods of nonviolent noncooperation with the government in order to secure the legitimate redress of the Indians' grievances. On the whole, he was quite effective, and his success became widely known in India. In 1914, when he returned, he did not plunge immediately into nationalist politics; rather, he toured India, surveying the situation and getting acquainted with his homeland and the nationalist leadership. In 1917, he began to move into a position of leadership in the movement. Gandhi recruited into the nationalist movement and his following many of the individuals who were to lead India to her freedom: the Nehrus, Sardar Patel, Pant, and many of the provincial leaders.

The Indian National Congress, the most important nationalist organization, radically changed its character and nature between 1917 and 1921. During this time, there were widespread disturbances, agitations, and campaigns culminating in the noncooperation movements of 1920 and 1921. The arena of conflict with the British government shifted from Westernized leadership in the coastal areas of Bombay and Bengal inland to less cosmopolitan leadership in the Punjab, Bihar, and Uttar Pradesh. Congress was successful in these areas not only in recruiting the Western-influenced elites who were smaller in number, proportionately, and more integrated into the rural societies than their counterparts on the coast but also in bringing three other crucial groups into the movement: the commercial classes of the towns and cities, the small but significant urban working class, and, most crucial, the substantial peasantry and the small landlords in the Ganges Valley, the key controllers of the countryside, with whom they formed an alliance.

In the 1920s and 1930s the British encouraged their allies, the larger landholders and princes, to enter politics and, through them, tried to control the mass of the population. But, as it became clear in 1937, when there were elections under the Constitution of 1935, the British and their Indian allies did not have control of the mass of the people. It was Congress and the nationalists who were able to control effectively the local power holders, who continued throughout the nineteenth century to wield power over the great mass of the local populations.

In the 1930s, the Muslim League, which was founded in 1906 and tended until the 1930s to be a small party advocating the interests of the Muslim population of India through the small Muslim elite classes of successful lawyers and landholders, began to grow spectacularly. Until the 1930s, the Muslim League's policies had been directed toward protection of Muslim rights. They tended to side with the British, who incorrectly charged Congress with merely expressing Hindu nationalism. In the early 1930s under the prodding of younger Muslim intellectuals and cultural nationalists, the Muslim League adopted the policy of seeking independence for a Muslim state, Pakistan, to be made up of the predominantly Muslim areas of the northwest. The Muslim League's greatest period of growth was after the elections of 1937, when their leaders were able to point to the fact that Congress's control meant essentially that Muslims were politically disadvantaged.

Throughout the 1920s, 1930s, and early 1940s, the British government carried on, at home, a long series of negotiations with representatives of all the major interests in India, nationalist and other. Administrative changes came rapidly after 1920, with an increasing number of Indians recruited for the higher civil service and officer ranks in the Indian army opened to Indians on a wide scale. At the provincial level, under the Government of India Acts of 1921 and 1935, increasing political participation of Indians as elected representatives developed, with Indians heading many of the branches of government.

The Indian National Congress government elected in 1937 resigned in 1939, and the Congress Party leaders, opposing any cooperation with the British, were jailed in 1942 during the Second World War and released at the end of the war. In the face of the mutiny of part of the Indian Navy late in 1945 and widespread civil disorders in 1946, both communal and directed against the British, the British Labor Government announced that India would become independent on August 15, 1947. After much negotiation, it was also announced that the country would be partitioned into Pakistan and India, a demand that the Muslim League had made its price for accepting independence.

India and Pakistan achieved independence in the summer of 1947 in the midst of large-scale movements of peoples: Hindus and Sikhs moving out of the West Punjab and Muslims moving out of Uttar Pradesh and East Punjab. There was widespread rioting and killing at the time of partition and after. The movement of peoples and killings spread to Bengal late in 1947 and in 1948. In addition, India and Pakistan fought a short but bitter war over Kashmir.

The two newly created states of India and Pakistan faced great difficulties, political, economic, and social. Large populations of refugees had to be absorbed; older and anachronistic political entities, represented by the princely states, had to be integrated. Since 1947, India and Pakistan have evolved in different political directions: India as a parliamentary democracy, and Pakistan with a strong central government that for the last ten years has been essentially a single-party dictatorship under Ayub Khan, a general of the Pakistan Army. As great as the problems faced by the new states were and continue to be and as close as disasters of many kinds have been at times, both India and Pakistan have developed stable and viable government structures. In a real sense, India and Pakistan were the first of the new nations, and although we continue to think of such as a "new nation," a full generation in both societies has come of age and has begun to see colonialism as a historic incident in a long history. Each country now legitimately thinks of itself politically as an "old nation."

CHAPTER TEN

Indian Social Structure and Culture: Introduction

Discussions of Indian society and culture always begin with a statement about the complexities and diversities actually found in India today. The most frequent statement made about India is that it is a land of "unity in diversity." It can be seen from the preceding chapters that the diversities flow from the geography and history of India, from the differing economic bases of its society, and from the differential rate of long-standing changes. In India, as in many "traditional" societies, there is a process of incorporation of change, in which one aspect of society or culture is not entirely replaced by another but in which change often leads to additions.instead of replacements. Any single statement that an anthropologist or sociologist may make about India is subject to a counterstatement. If one says that residence is virilocal, someone else quickly points out that, in Kerala and in some parts of Assam, inheritance, even today, tends to be through the mother's line and a male goes to live with or is closely associated with the family of his wife.

Statements that are statistically valid, however, can be made about aspects of Indian social structure. Inheritance of rights and property is through the male line. Most Indians are socialized in households where there are adults in addition to their own mothers and fathers. Statistical statements can be made about the nature of village structure, caste, family, local political structures, urban middle-class families, and so forth. The range and variation in institutions or clusters of social relations can be noted or described.

Much of what follows is a description of the major aspects of Indian society of the last twenty years, and some suggestion of how the major aspects of the society and culture are changing. To understand contemporary Indian society and culture, one begins, not with a statistical or even normative picture of the institutions and values, the social relationships, and the expected behaviors, but with the underlying assumptions that seem to pervade the culture.

Most observers of Indian society, I think, accept Louis Dumont's view that, when one penetrates the bewildering proliferation of social forms and cultural expressions in India, he finds that most relations and most values come down to a question of hierarchy. One can find that there are no peer relations in the family. The father is dominant over his sons; males are dominant over females; older brothers over younger. This stratification is frequently symbolized in the forms of address and reference found in the kinship terminology in the family. An older brother may address a younger brother by name, but a younger brother addresses an older brother by a kin term. Few behaviors in the family indicate an equality. A boy rises when his father comes into the room. He stops talking. If he is smoking or eating, he stops. He does not speak until spoken to. The hierarchy spreads from the family into families who claim descent from a common ancestor and who are in the same lineage. Some families, because they are descended from a younger brother, are slightly lower in social status than other families within the lineage. Genealogical as distinct from chronological age determines formal behavior among members of a lineage. For example, when two members who know they are of the same lineage meet, they immediately determine their genealogical relationship so that they may use the right behavior and form of address in formal situations. Members of lineages are tied to other lineages through marriage, but, by and large, marriage within the marrying groups of a caste does not establish peer relations between the two families who have established marriage ties. Generally speaking, the boy's family, by accepting a girl from another family, establishes a higher status within the marrying group than the family that gives the girl. When a member of the girl's family comes to visit at the household of the boy, he is made to feel that his status is lower than that of the family he is visiting.

Greetings also symbolize the hierarchy central to the social structure. In northern India, there is a range of gestures and phrases that is appropriate to one's status and to the status of the person being greeted. A person of lower status, whether that status is based on caste, age, or genealogical connection, is the first to greet the person of higher status. The greeting may be a salute, like a gesture with a slight bow, or a greeting using both hands, palm to palm, in front of the body. The height of the hands in front of the chest, the lower part of the face, or the forehead, is adjusted to the status of the person being greeted. A person of lower status frequently adds an horonific title to the phrase of greeting to a higher-status person. The grammar of salutation and return salutation graphically symbolizes the hierarchic relations between individuals and groups.

One's position in a seated group is another symbolization of the hierarchic nature of social relations. The principal article of furniture used for sitting or reclining is a cot (*charpāī*) made of rope strung on a wooden frame. There are higher- and lower-ranking ends to the cot. The foot of the cot, where there is small, tight webbing as in the main part of the cot, is lower than the head or high-ranking end. If four or five people are sitting on or near a cot, one can quickly see the formal relations among them. The eldest person, with membership in the highest-ranked caste group in the area, sits in the highest-status place at the head of the cot and the others are graded down from this position, either sitting on the cot or sitting or squatting on the ground around it.

It is easiest to see hierarchy in the social realm, but it has cultural expression in the great concern felt by most Indians about *pollution* and *purity*. People, many materials, objects, and social states are ranked on a continuum from purity to pollution. Polluted states can be transmitted from one object or person to other objects and persons. Some persons can pollute pure things or purify polluted things. States of pollution and purity may be permanent or transitory.

The purity-pollution continuum may be illustrated by the hierarchy involved in the categories of food and the processing, giving, and receiving of food. It is possible to think of food in five categories. Raw food—that which is given as gifts or as part of wages—can be given by anyone to anyone. It can be considered either the purest of food or neutral. With the next three kinds of food—that fried in oil, that boiled in water, and food of either category from someone else's plate (garbage)— who has done the cooking and handling, either in serving or presenting, makes a great difference in the degree of purity or pollution. Food cooked or fried in oil (*pakka*) by a Brahman can usually be eaten or accepted by anyone. Food cooked in water can be eaten only by someone of one's own group or someone who accepts an inferior status to that group. Garbage, the leavings on the plates of others, is usually taken only by very low-status persons. The final food category includes carrion and feces. Both are considered to be highly polluting. Some low castes eat carrion beef—now eschewed even by those who, a few generations back, ate it—and the grain found in the feces of animals. In addition to the relative purity and pollution of the five major categories of foodstuffs— raw, cooked in oil, cooked in water, garbage, and carrion and feces—

there are several other kinds of food. In some respects, the purest food of all is *prasad*, that which has been offered in a ritual fashion to a sacred object, such as the representation of a deity in a temple, and then is taken and distributed for consumption.

Food within any category may range widely in its purity. Generally vegetables and grains are purer than meat. Within the meat category, the range is from eggs (the least polluted of "meats") through fish, chicken, goats and sheep, wild pork, domestic pork and, finally, water buffalo and beef, the most polluting of all meats. Some vegetable foods are considered "stronger" than others. For example, for the Havic Brahmans of Mysore, onions and garlic, the food that resembles meat in color, such as pumpkins, radishes, tomatoes, and carrots, are considered inappropriate to Brahmanical status and are less pure or more polluting than other vegetable foods.[1]

Human beings, too, can be in relative states of purity or pollution. Some people, usually termed *Untouchables,* are thought by others in the society to be in a permanent state of pollution. In northern India, they are not literally untouchable, that is, one is not automatically polluted by their touch; but in certain situations and in relation to certain substances, particularly food and water, their touch can be polluting. A person belonging to an untouchable group within a village is not allowed to go into the area within a higher-caste person's house in which the *chula* (the small earthen stove) is located. This area is usually distinguished by a fresh plaster of mud and cow dung. Similarly, in most situations, a high-caste person does not accept cooked food or water from a person defined as an untouchable, because the water or food would transmit the pollution permanent and inherent in the person of the untouchable. In southern India, in the past and in rural areas today, the touch of an untouchable was polluting, and under certain circumstances some untouchables literally had to be kept at a distance. Any person, however, can be in a state of pollution or impurity. The period can range from a few hours to many days and can be of differing intensity. A woman who is menstruating or a man whose father has died can be polluting. In the case of a father's death, the state of pollution may last up to a month, and the touch of the mourner may be as defiling as that of an untouchable.

In southern India, where concerns about states of pollution and purity are somewhat more intense, three states of purity are ritually recognized:

---

[1] Edward B. Harper, "Ritual Pollution as an Integrator of Caste and Religion," in Edward B. Harper (ed.), *Religion in South Asia* (Seattle: University of Washington Press, 1964), p. 155. The whole article is an excellent discussion of the concept of pollution and its effects on behavior of a southern Indian Brahman caste.

ritually impure, ritually pure or normal, or lacking ritual status. One is usually in a state lacking ritual status, that is, one is working in the fields or going about his usual activities. To become ritually impure or to have pollution, one must engage in "a ritually defiling act or . . . have contact with a source of pollution." [2] For example, one must have been touched by an untouchable or have come into contact with a defiling substance, such as human feces. Becoming ritually pure is necessary in order to carry out rituals. Under most circumstances, bathing puts a male into a state of ritual purity. However, the act of bathing and getting into clean clothes is in itself, as described by Harper, a very complicated affair:

> To become *madi* (ritually pure) a person must have a complete bath, including pouring water over the hair, and the water should be drawn from a pure source by a Brahmin who is not in *muttuchettu* (ritually impure). If cotton clothing is worn it must have been washed by someone in *madi* (a state of ritual purity) and to remain in a state of *madi* (ritual purity), the wearer must not touch any cloth which is not *madi*.[3]

Another underlying fact in Indian society that must be grasped is that India is a group-based, not an individual-based society. Most action and behavior in which an individual Indian engages are in relation to and mediated by the various groups to which he belongs. Most of these groups are ascriptive; one is born into them. The judgments made of his actions by himself and others are in relation to the groups to which he belongs. The groups can be viewed as the circles of an onion, with the center circle being the family, which, for a male, usually means the household in which he grows up and to which his bride comes when he is married. Even if he does not live in a household with his father, brothers, and other male kin when he is an adult, to others, this group is still his family. The family to which he belongs is related genealogically to other families who live close by, and although at times their relations may be antagonistic or even hostile, the tie binding a small number of families, related through the male line, is significant. As a working or landholding group, the families have ritual obligations to one another. A larger number of families may be tied in a lineage: a group of males, in most parts of India, who recognize descent from a known ancestor. For upper landholding castes in much of India, this may be an important tie, and such a lineage may extend over dozens of villages creating an important political and social unit.

[2] *Ibid.*, p. 152.
[3] *Ibid.*, p. 153.

A male grows up recognizing kinship, real or fictive, with other males who are part of his *biradari* (local caste group), which may or may not coincide with the lineage. The *biradari* is the basic unit of the caste system. It is exogamous in that one always marries outside of his *biradari* and considers the males in it of his own age his brothers, the women of his age his sisters, older men as fathers, and older women as mothers. Marriage within the *biradari* would be considered incestuous. The *biradari* is the functional level of the caste system. It may have a head who is recognized as able to act for members of the *biradari;* it may jointly own some property, such as large cooking pots, tents, or ritual objects; it may have formal machinery of government and social control. The membership of a particular exogamous section of a caste, the *biradari,* is fairly easy to determine. Members have a face-to-face knowledge of each other and extend kin terms to each other. The members of a *biradari* establish marriage ties with other such units that form a much wider circle of recognized caste fellows and potential mates and cognatic kin. This unit is called the *jati* in northern India. It is endogamous; often it is named, has a myth of origin, and sometimes a sacred spot or temple. It also has shared stories and legends about its history.

On occasion, leaders of various *biradaris* meet to determine rules concerning behavior or adjudicate disputes that arise between members of different *biradaris* within the *jati*. Enforcement of regulations or judgments made by leaders of the *jati* is left to the *biradaris* usually, but since the *jati* eventually controls the right of any member of a *biradari* to marry and since he must marry out of his own *biradari* into another one in the *jati,* a threat by other *biradaris* to prevent marriages into a recalcitrant *biradari* can often be used to control the behavior of its members.

The *biradari,* the exogamous section of a caste, and the *jati,* the endogamous section, are the functional levels of a caste system from the point of view of its members. But there are two other levels recognized by Indians and observers of the caste system. Within broad regions— the Upper Ganges Valley, for example, there are *jatis* all roughly of the same status, often with a general name applied to them, such as Lohar (carpenter) or Ahir (cattle herder). These *jatis* follow the same traditional occupation and are lumped together as a caste (*jat*). This is not a functioning group but a caste category, much as we might say someone is lower middle class—a very general description. Often when two strangers from different parts of a region meet, they identify themselves by one of these caste category names. Finally, there are ideological categories in the system called *varnas*—the Brahmans, Kshatriyas, Vysayas, and Sutras. These four categories include all but the untouchable castes. The *varnas* set a very broad explanatory framework, laying out duties and rights and characteristics that members of the *varnas* are assumed to have. The *varna* categories also are important, as we shall see, when a caste tries to change its status, because its members claim membership in one of the two top *varnas:* Brahman or Kshatriya. Sociologically, in terms of determining group membership, it is only the *biradari* and the *jati* that are important. These, in sociological terms, are groups, since they have a concrete reality and a known or knowable membership and structure.

For most rural Indians, about 80 percent of the population, an identification with a village is also important, and for upper- and medium-rank castes this identification represents an important loyalty and allegiance. Most males spend the majority of their lives in one village. Even when someone moves away to a city or to another area, he maintains ties with his natal place. Although his ties to his family, his extended kin group, and his lineage, his *biradari,* and his *jati* are crucial, he also identifies and has a series of structured relations with members of his village who are not of his family lineage and *biradari.*

The social ties that one is born with set obligations, rights, and duties. An Indian frequently submerges his individual concern with the concerns of a group. His identity is determined by group membership; the ties are there and continue to be there after he dies. The ties are not equally or continuously operative but are situational and contingent. One's immediate situation determines which tie should be emphasized, which identity is crucial, which action affects the group. Rural Indians are constantly engaged in quick and minute shiftings of ties and identities, depending on current situations. Often the ties and identities conflict; when a brother quarrels with a brother, a *biradari* member quarrels with a *biradari* mate and seeks help in another *jati* in the village, or a village splits into contending factions. The ties cross-cut and ramify. Although, theoretically, there should be a hierarchy of allegiances and values, with the family being primary, the activities of daily life blur the ideal allegiances.

Underlying the social and cultural system, then, are the attributes of hierarchy, purity and pollution, and group-based ties. With these attributes in mind, we now can turn to an examination of the structure and institutions of Indian society, with the caveat once again that every statement about any aspect of Indian society is subject to qualification.

INDIAN SOCIAL STRUCTURE AND CULTURE: FAMILY

In the past, social scientists and other writers on India wrote as if there were only one kind of Indian family: a joint or extended family. The characteristics of this ideal joint family were summarized by Irawati

Karve in the following terms: "A joint family is a group of people who generally live under one roof, who eat food cooked at one hearth, who hold property in common and who participate in common family worship and are related to each other as some particular kind of kindred." [4] These characteristics define the Indian joint family. During intensive study of Indians by sociologists and anthropologists, however, a number of questions have arisen about the prevalence, nature, and direction of change in Indian family structure.

In two recent and important papers, Pauline Kolenda has surveyed and analyzed a wide range of data gathered by anthropologists on family structures in India.[5] She has shown that there is a wide range of regional, caste, and perhaps, economic differences in the kind of family structure found in India. The older categories of *nuclear* (a family or household consisting of a man, his wife, and their children) or *joint* household (made up of three generations: a grandfather, grandmother, their son or sons, their wives, and children) or *collateral joint* family (two or more brothers, their spouses, and children) are too simple to encompass the actual range of structural type found among families in India. A further complicating factor is that families exist through time. A nuclear family can become a joint family if, when the sons grow up, they decide to remain together; a collateral joint family (two or more brothers or cousins) can turn into a full three-generation joint family. Similarly, a joint family can break into constituent nuclear families. Anthropologists following Meyer Fortes's work on West Africa now recognize that most family systems have a development cycle with a regular pattern of buildup and breakdown in structure going on all the time. The fact of the family development cycle has made it very difficult with anthropological data, which tends to report family forms at a particular time, to assess any direction of change in the Indian context. We do not know whether or not the joint family system is breaking up or if there are more nuclear families now than there were in the past, as we do not know how many of a particular type there were at any particular place in the past. I think most anthropologists assume that there may not have been any statistically significant change in family types in the recent past.

---

[4] Irawati Karve, "Kinship Organization in India," *Deccan College Monograph Series,* 11 (Poona, India: Post-graduate and Research Institute, 1953), 10.

[5] Pauline Kolenda, "Region, Caste and Family: A Comparative Study of the Indian 'Joint' Family," in Milton Singer and Bernard S. Cohn (eds.), *Social Structure and Social Change in India* (Chicago: Viking Fund Publications in Anthropology, 43, 1968), and "Regional Differences in Indian Family Structure," in Robert I. Crane (ed.), "Regions and Regionalism in South Asian Studies: An Exploratory Study," *Monograph and Occasional Paper Series Program in Comparative Studies on Southern Asia,* 5 (Duke University, 1967).

To grasp the nature of family life in rural India, which to some extent is the predominant model for all India, one starts with a household. The minimal operating definition of a household for much of India is those who share the food of a single hearth. Usually, this means a grouping, other than individuals who live alone, of at least an adult male, an adult female who is his wife, and their children. When this unit is more complex, kinship is usually traced through the male line, although in Kerala, among some castes, it is traced along the female line, and in some parts of southern India where cross-cousin marriage and uncle-niece marriage are permitted, ties may be through both lines. The household, then, can consist of a variety of kin groupings.

Sharing of food, no matter which kin groupings are involved, usually includes joint holding of property, whether land, a house, furniture, tools, or goods. The property may be considered joint and all males may have a potential share in the property, but its use tends to be vested in the head, usually the oldest male. His authority, theoretically, is absolute over the property, and presumably, he makes the major decisions regarding actions of members of the household.

Except in Kerala and in some castes in southern India, the males grow up in the villages and houses of their fathers. Females who come in as spouses for members of the household grow up elsewhere, but usually not a great distance away. By Western standards, marriage of girls takes place at a relatively young age. Even when a girl goes through the marriage ceremony at the age of eleven or twelve, the marriage is not usually consummated until she is fifteen or so. The age of marriage for girls in India is rising at present.

Early marriage for girls serves a very obvious function, particularly if the girl is moving into a household in a caste or region that has the tradition of joint households. She comes in at an early age, gets socialized to the norms and values of her husband's household, and is less independent than a woman who marries at a later age. Socialization to the values of the family she marries into is important in terms of one of the structural strains built into this kind of family structure. The ideology in a joint household system is to make the tie among the males of a particular generation strong. The brothers must form a tightly knit group if the family is to remain joint. The development of a strong tie to a wife may endanger this, because the husband might put his tie to his wife above his tie to his brothers. Customarily, there is considerable social distance between husband and wife at the formal level. Husband and wife do not call each other or refer to each other by name or kinship terms but by the relationship to their children. Hence, a wife is referred to by her husband as the mother of so-and-so, her eldest son, if she has one. The use of the eldest son's name also symbolizes one of the main functions of the wife—to provide male heirs to continue the family line. A wife does not eat with her husband, who eats alone or with other adult males in the family. Only after she has served him his meal does a wife eat with the other women of the household and with siblings and cousins. The small child is likely to be cared for by a number of adult women; in addition to his mother, his father's mother, his father's brother's wife, or the wife of one of his own older brothers. As an infant, for all but nursing, a child is handed around. All who are not burdened with other responsibilities take a hand with the care of the young child. Slightly older siblings and cousins, particularly females, take a major share in watching, playing with, and caring for the child. In an Indian village, a typical sight is a girl, at least eight or nine years old but not yet married out of the village, carrying a small sibling on her hip almost everywhere she goes. The child, then, in earliest years, grows up in an environment including a number of parental figures and a number of siblings. Even in a nuclear household, it is likely that the child, from an early age, is cared for by relatives or neighbors, so that structurally, although his household may not have more than a mother and father in it, the culture of the joint household pervades the early years of the child.

The pervasiveness of the joint family culture, of course, is facilitated by the nature of the house itself. In a climate in which there is little need for shelter during the day, except during the rainy season, the house by itself is not necessarily the locus of many activities that Westerners think of as taking place in the house. Many Indians, at least the males, sleep outside, bathe outside, and spend their leisure time outside. Many household tasks, such as preparing and grinding grain, also take place outside. The house is used for storage, as a kitchen, as a place in which women sleep, and as a place in which men and women have sexual relations. Other than these, activities for men and some for women take place on the veranda and in the space in front of the house, which is the main locus of family activities.

It is usually thought that the joint family is essentially a social form associated with the rural segment of a traditional society and found among landholding groups. This relationship would seem to follow if the data from the Ganges Valley are taken as typical. The traditional landholding groups, such as the Rajputs, Bhuminars, and Jats in the Ganges Valley, are our point of reference. In other parts of India, however, this is not generally the case. The Marathas of western India, some of the landholding groups of Bengal, and many of the landholding groups of southern India do not emphasize the ideology of the joint family and the extension of this ideology into corporate lineage segments. A military tradition rather than landholding as such may be the crucial variable in determining which groups emphasize the joint family ideology.

Landholders and military groups are not the only ones for whom the joint family is economically functional for keeping property together and, providing a pool of labor and supervisory personnel. The joint family is a highly functional form of organization for artisans and merchants as well.

In artisan groups, in both villages and towns, joint family living is found. I. P. Desai, who carried out a study of family types and functions in a small Indian city, found considerable variation among artisan groups in relation to the degree of jointness in their family structure.[6] Blacksmiths had low degrees of jointness and potters had relatively high degree of jointness. Other artisan and service groups in the sample Desai studied were too small to indicate anything about the distribution of family types. It is clear from logical analysis, though, that artisans, if they need a labor pool or pooling of tools, capital, or materials for their work, find a joint family functional.

Among merchant groups, Desai found a fairly high percentage of families with a high degree of jointness. Again, for merchants who need to concentrate capital or differentiate business specialties, the joint family seems to be functional as well. In the past and in the present, the family firm is one of the principal means of carrying on business in India, even for very extensive operations.

When one views the functions of a joint family, rather than mere co-residence as the criterion for establishing jointness, it seems that the joint family is highly functional for business groups even when members of the family live widely scattered over India. Brothers or cousins, in effect, act as agents of family business in different cities and towns but still operate with a common purse and with a common decision-making locus for their business activities. It is often argued that a joint family is antithetical to the development of business and entrepreneurial activities. It has been assumed that, in a family system that allows members to have a claim on the family purse and an automatic share in the property of the family, a situation might develop in which a few members would be burdened with the support of many inactive members. In reality, this does not seem to happen. Rather the males of the joint business family form a corporation, have mutual trust, and have the advantage of a pool of capital.

One of the most persistent social science theories is that modern education, industrial employment, work in the free professions, and white-

[6] I. P. Desai, *Some Aspects of Family in Mahura: A Sociological Study of Jointness in a Small Town* (New York: Asia Publishing House, 1964).

collar employment deal a death blow to an extended family system. The theory evolves from assumptions about the nature of the history of the Western family, where it has been assumed that, at some time, in Western Europe and Great Britain, there was a large extended family system that broke apart under the impact of the commercial and industrial revolutions. Recent work by social historians has cast considerable doubt on the theory. Recent research seems to indicate that the nuclear family, certainly as far back as the Middle Ages in England, was the predominant type. It has been assumed that structurally, because of spatial mobility, and ideologically, because of the development of modern education, economic opportunity, and the growth of individualism inherent in modern cultures, the joint family could not survive and that, particularly in modern urban settings, nuclear families would predominate.

What evidence there is concerning the Indian family under modern urban conditions does not lead to clear conclusions. The most complete study of the Indian family under modern conditions is that of sociologist Aileen D. Ross.[7] Through questionnaires and case studies, she studied 157 individuals, mainly of high castes—Brahmans constituted two-thirds of her sample and middle-rank castes, Okkaligas and Reddis the remaining part—in Bangalore, Mysore, which is a large city with a significant amount of modern industrial activity. The sample is biased in favor of those in the modern segment of the economy and does not include any of the working-class population of the city. Ross used a very narrow definition of jointness in her study, relying on household composition as the main criterion, but Desai tried to include a wide range of factors in establishing his criteria for jointness. Ross's data show that, at the time of her study (the late 1950s), 37 percent of those interviewed were living in joint households and 40 percent had grown up in joint households.[8] It is impossible to tell, since there are no comparative or historical data on the groups from which these urban dwellers were recruited, whether these percentages represent any change brought about by urban living or by variations, in time, in the pattern of the distribution of family types in Mysore. It can be seen, though, that a significant number of educated middle-class families in a modern Indian city live in joint families.

There is much anecdotal evidence, in the form of casual observations and in novels, such as those of R. K. Narayan and Ruth Jabvala, that even in the modern cities and in highly educated classes engaged in modern occupations, both the structure and the ideology of the joint

---

[7] *The Hindu Family in Its Urban Setting* (Toronto: University of Toronto Press, 1961).

[8] Calculations based on data in *Ibid.*, pp. 36, 37.

family persist. Most middle-class urban families support relatives in their households for long periods of time, as dependents or while they attend school or look for work. The family in the city is a center of freely given assistance for rural relatives. Similarly, income derived from urban employment, even from long-established urban families, is often remitted to the families still living in the villages. Property held in the village is still considered joint property, shared with the family living in the city. Sometimes a pattern is consciously worked out among brothers holding some property in a village, in which one or more brothers and their families remain in the village to work and manage the family property, while other brothers seek their fortune in business or government service in the cities. Although some brothers may establish long-term residence with their families in cities and towns, they still consider themselves part of a joint family located in the village, with children from both village and town spending long periods of time with their father's brothers' families.

The ideology of the joint family often persists in unlikely situations. Myron Weiner, a political scientist, found in his study of opposition parties and their structure that groups in parties frequently have the authority pattern of a joint family in which the group leader is treated as the head of a joint family.[9] In a wide range of situations, the ideology, the culture, and the feeling tone of the joint family seem to persist and affect many situations long after the structure of the joint family has disappeared.

[9] Myron Weiner, *Party Politics in India* (Princeton, N. J.: Princeton University Press, 1957), p. 238–39.

CHAPTER ELEVEN

Indian Social Structure and Culture: Caste

The institution taken as the hallmark of Indian society is caste. The study of caste—its origins, structure, history, and functions—has engaged scholars and observers of India for generations. There is no generally accepted single definition of the caste system, but there is widespread agreement on its attributes. The caste system consists of a number of groups, recruited by birth; membership in the group determines many behaviors, expectations, obligations, and evaluations of individuals and determines their access to the valued statuses and activities in society. Status in the system is ascriptive and, for the individual, unchanging as far as group-determined activities are concerned. There is a hierarchy in the system, leading to the ranking of groups. Marriage is within the group. Sometimes particular roles, either negatively or positively valued, are the exclusive privilege of group members—priestly roles, certain craft activities, and service functions.

To summarize, caste membership is by birth. Caste status is ascriptive and unchanging for the individual. Castes are endogamous; they are ranked within a local system. Underlying the caste are values associated with ideas of purity and pollution.

In recent years there has been considerable argument about the use of the word "caste" as a term applied generally to relatively closed stratification systems found outside Indian civilization.[1]

---

[1] For recent arguments on the question, see Gerald Berreman, "Stratification, Pluralism and Interaction: A Comparative Analysis of Caste," in A. V. S. de Reuck and Julie Knight (eds.), *Ciba Foundation Symposium on Caste and Race: Comparative Approaches* (London: J. and A. Churchill, 1967), pp. 45–73; Berreman, "Caste

Sociologists and others have long used the word "caste," which is not the indigenous word applied to the system in India but a word first used by the Portuguese to mean "breed or type" and applied by them to the closed groups found in India. Conceptually, caste is used to describe any relatively closed stratification system in which recruitment to its constituent parts is by birth and in which there is little movement from one closed group to another, either through intermarriage or through individual mobility. Caste in these terms is at one end of a continuum, and a class-based society is at the other. Clearly, caste can be used in this sense for the comparative study of stratification systems, either in rigorous or common-sense terms, and eventually such usage may help to illuminate stratification systems generally. But thus far, it is still hard to see whether the discussion has added much to an understanding of the caste system in India. In this essay, the word "caste," unless otherwise specified, refers to the particular aspects of the system in India.

CASTE AS KINSHIP

From the vantage point of a village and one family in that village, rather than from an overall view of the caste system of India in descriptive or analytical terms, caste can be seen initially as an extension of the kinship system. Members of the first-level unit in the system comprise what is termed the *biradari,* or the "band of brothers." There is real or fictive extension of kinship to all members of the *biradari.* Within it, members are treated as relatives within age categories; that is, all members of the same generation are regarded as brothers, older generations as fathers or mothers. The *biradari* is exogamous, much as the family is exogamous in northern India. For middle- and lower-rank castes, the *biradari* is usually a corporate group.

Members meet frequently on an informal or formal basis. All members of the *biradari* are represented at life-cycle rites. The heads of the various households making up the *biradari* are represented at discussions or meetings (*panchayats*) called to adjudicate disputes or to regulate behaviors of members.

The span or ground coverage of a *biradari* is a function of demography. If many members of a particular *biradari* live in one or two villages, the boundary of the *biradari* is of narrow span. This is true in northern India

---

in Cross-cultural Perspective," in G. DeVos and H. Wagatsuma (eds.), *Japan's Invisible Race: Caste in Culture and Personality* (Berkeley: University of California Press, 1966), pp. 275–324; for an argument stressing the uniqueness of the Indian context for caste, Edmund Leach, Introduction to *Aspects of Caste in South India, Ceylon and Northwest Pakistan* (Cambridge: Cambridge University Press, 1960).

for the untouchable laboring castes, such as Chamars, and some of the middle-rank agricultural castes, such as Koeris or Ahirs. Usually, few members of the artisan and serving castes, such as potters, blacksmiths, and washermen, are found in a particular village. The span of the *biradari* in this situation stretches over dozens of villages.

It is generally true that upper castes, both priestly and landed, tend not to be well organized into *biradaris*. In the more distant past, in the eighteenth and early nineteenth centuries, there is evidence that the upper castes were well organized at the *biradari* level in terms of internal management, particularly where landholding lineages were concerned. But for Rajputs, Jats, and Khandaits, the organization emphasized the lineage and clan structure of the group rather than the caste structure.

The *biradari* level of an individual is the only clearly bounded unit in the system. The next level can usually be analytically differentiated as the *jati* level—the group into which members of a *biradari* marry. Sometimes, however, clear geographic features, such as rivers or hills, define the boundary of the *jati* for individuals in the *biradari*. The tie between the *biradari* and the *jati* levels in the system is through marriage or through one's mother's family. In the north, effective cognizance of the *jati* boundary varies from family to family within a biradari.

For most castes, representatives from the constituent *biradaris* of the *jati* rarely have occasion to meet for any social or ritual purpose. The *jati*, in a structural sense, is a system of actual or potential networks of *affinal* and *cognatic* kinship ties. Often the *jati* has cultural characteristics that its members believe set them off from others in the region who have the same *jat* (caste category). Often the *jati* is named, may follow food restrictions not followed by other *jatis* in the *jat*, and may have a deity or hero associated with the *jati*. Above all, the members believe themselves to be different from others of the *jat* but not of their *jati*. Effective social control at the *jati* level is exercised through *biradaris* and through kin networks binding particular families and *biradaris* in the *jati*. The *jati* is frequently called the *subcaste* in older literature concerning the caste system.

CASTE AS CULTURAL AND OCCUPATIONAL CATEGORIES

Most of the terms for particular castes, such as Lohar, Okkaliga, Nayar, Kayastha, and several hundred others, refer to the *jat* level in the system, which is a categorical level. Throughout macroregions such as the Upper Ganges Valley of West Bengal or highland Orissa are found members of different *jatis* following roughly the same customs and frequently the same occupations. Others in the area call them by a common name that does not refer to the subcaste or *jati* name and regard them as being of the same *jat*. Members of these *jatis*, too, when pressed, agree that members of different *jatis* can be grouped together as one *jat* and sometimes accept the title or name applied to them. With very few exceptions, until recently (the turn of the century), there was no effective social organization at this level of the system. It was a cultural category rather than a structural unit.

There has been much confusion about caste and occupation. It must first be understood that the primary occupation of most rural Indians, in the present as well as in the past, is caste-free agriculture. All castes could follow most agricultural pursuits, and most did so. Even craftsmen and artisans were usually agriculturalists as well. Particular castes, such as Rajputs and Brahmans, may have had customary prohibitions against some agricultural tasks like plowing, but they could and did do every other kind of agricultural work. Caste occupations such as blacksmithing, pottery making, weaving, and priestcraft were restrictive, mainly in the sense that not everyone who had one of these occupations as a tradition followed it. But particularly in the ritual component—and most occupations have a ritual or ideological component—only members of such occupational categories could properly carry out the occupation. Even today, most blacksmiths are of the blacksmith caste, most weavers of the weaving caste, most cattleherds of the cattleherd caste. Those crafts or occupations which require considerable skill and training are usually restricted to members of the caste, because others would have little opportunity to learn the necessary skills. In the present as in the past, some parts of craft occupations that do not require great skill—the making of tiles for roofs, for example—are sometimes done by general laborers.

Caste occupations often have a negative component. Some castes are forced to do defiling or degrading work. Chamars, whose traditional occupation was leather working, skinning, and tanning, by extension are still responsible throughout most of northern India for the removal of dead animals, and female Chamars are midwives. Chamars cannot choose to carry out their traditional jobs without great difficulty and often direct violence.

Many people in the nineteenth century believed, and some even today believe, that the association of caste with occupations would be a detriment to the introduction of new occupations and roles. This has proved to be a myth, as Morris D. Morris has convincingly shown; neither in the cotton textile industry nor in the steel industry was caste a factor in the ability to recruit a labor force. Brahmans in the nineteenth century willingly went into modern medicine, although it meant dealing with corpses, dissection, and other activities normally thought to be highly defiling. Modern office and administrative skills were quickly found to be a function of education and training rather than caste occupation. Chauffeurs and drivers, mechanics and machine spinners did not and have not turned out to be new castes, as some of the British observers of the caste system quaintly believed. Caste and caste-based roles have not turned out to be a particular problem in the development of a modern economy in India.

What relationship there is between caste and modern occupations is a function rather of differential access to educational opportunity and the working of nepotism along caste lines. A rough correlation exists in the modern economy between caste status in a broad sense and occupations. If one looks at the industrial and white-collar labor force in a city, one finds very generally that untouchables are in the lowest occupational categories, such as unskilled laborers, rickshaw pullers, and coolies. Lower-rank and middle-rank caste members are found as semiskilled or skilled laborers and the upper castes as skilled laborers, white-collar workers, or managers in the system. It can be argued, though, that this is more a function of educational levels than of caste alone. In the rural economy there is a correlation based on income, caste status, traditions of literacy, and education. Caste does operate in a very broad way to influence recruitment into modern occupations, but this is different from saying that modern occupations are based solely on caste.

Caste is operative in another sense in the modern occupational structure. A particular office or section of a factory may have a high percentage of members of a certain caste or *jati*, because workers are often recruited for jobs along kin, clan, and caste lines. In the Indian context, one is very likely to hire or recommend for hiring someone he knows or can find out about, and one is likely to know more about one's caste fellows than about noncaste fellows. The clustering of members of particular *jatis* can also facilitate cooperation in the work situation, because customs, attitudes, and beliefs are similar.

The government and large firms are very much aware of the general and specific danger that can flow from a situation in which members of a particular caste or *jati* control jobs. The government is strongly attacking the problem by investing heavily in order to make education available to all citizens regardless of caste, religion, or sex. Increasingly, most government jobs are recruited by open competition, except that members of depressed castes are given some advantages in the form of access to particular posts. This action—increasing educational opportunity and reserving posts—should allow more of the depressed and lower castes to make their way into more prestigious and higher-paying positions.

CASTES AS POLITICAL AND VOLUNTARY ASSOCIATIONS

In premodern India, there was a close relationship between caste and the political order. Under Hindu law, it was the king's responsibility to prevent the "confusion of castes." Evidence indicates that he could change caste status, create new castes, and establish caste precedence and rank. In functional terms, the king was usually thought of as the great ruler over large empires, but through much of India's history he was the ruler over small territories. The king had the authority and power to maintain the caste system. Ultimately, he could physically coerce those over whom he had power. The caste system, like any stratification system, requires groups with power to maintain the system. This power has been provided, not by Brahmans, not by sacred authority, but by political power.

Anthropologist Eric Miller, referring to the political structure of Malabar (Kerala) in premodern times, pointed out that in society the effective organization was a relatively small-scale state (the *nad*) in which most ties were vertical to the head of *nad*, rather than horizontal to one's caste fellows over wide ranges of territory. It was the vertical tie that proved crucial. Most marriage ties, except for the ruling groups, the Nayars and the Brahmans, were within the *nad*. Economic relations for most of the territory were within the *nad*, and most networks were within the territory.[2] The model that Miller suggests for Malabar can be found in much of the rest of India.

In hill states, as late as the end of the nineteenth century, the king was still called upon to settle disputes arising both within and between castes. He had the authority to prevent other castes or sections within castes from serving or having relations with castes or sections of castes being punished. In effect, the king could "outcaste" sections of castes.

Along with the political changes coming in the wake of the establishment of British rule was a rapid decline in the power of the local chief rulers and lineages to exert any widespread force within their territories or across territorial boundaries. Ties that had been essentially vertical could now be expanded horizontally, and so, in the nineteenth century, both the identification with one's *jat* and the opportunity for interaction expanded. Members of the *jat* have become a more important aspect at the *jat* level of the caste during the nineteenth and twentieth centuries than ever before. What were actually voluntary associations made up of

[2] Eric Miller, "Caste and Territory in Malabar," *The American Anthropologist*, 56, (1954), 410–20.

members of particular *jats* began to develop. These are called caste *sabhas*. The caste *sabhas*, once organized, offered scholarships to schools, provided living quarters for members of the *jats* at colleges, published journals, helped in the arranging of marriages, lobbied when necessary with the government, and even fought cases in the courts when it seemed that the status of the caste was being harmed by governmental or private actions. The caste network within a *jat* could expand with the rise of modern means of communication, of printing, the mails, and cheap, rapid transportation in the form of trains. With the introduction of electoral politics in some areas, the caste *sabhas* became politicized, helping candidates of their own *jat* to contest elections and directing appeals to members of the *jat* to support their caste fellows. Voluntary caste associations were important internal arenas for developing political skills and followings that could be used on the wider stage, regionally, and, in a few instances, even nationally. Another paradox has followed from the change of political structure. Direct authority over relations among castes has become much more local and is now essentially vested in the hands of the dominant caste in a particular village or small group of villages. "For a caste to be dominant, it should own a sizeable amount of the arable land locally available, have strength of numbers and occupy a high place in the local hierarchy." [3] In effect, the dominant landholding caste in a village or local area now plays the role that the king formerly played in relation to the caste system.

THE CASTE SYSTEM

Thus far, the discussion has centered on caste as a component of the system and not on how castes interact or are tied in with one another to form a system. To see the caste system in operation, it is easiest to look at a large, multicaste village with a resident dominant caste. Not all Indian villages have these characteristics, but in almost every region of India one finds such villages along with smaller villages with one or two castes, with tribal villages, towns, and cities. The model of the caste system that anthropologists have recently developed is based on the multicaste village.

Within a village, there is considerable face-to-face interaction as well as knowledge about residents in the local area. Since a person's *jati* is

[3] M. N. Srinivas, *Social Change in Modern India* (Berkeley: University of California Press, 1966), p. 10. Also see M. N. Srinivas, "The Dominant Caste in Rampura," *The American Anthropologist*, 61 (February, 1959), 1–16, and Adrian Mayer, "The Dominant Caste in a Region of Central India," *Southwestern Journal of Anthropology*, 14 (1958), 407–27.

known, the first question that arises in relation to a caste system in other settings (How do you know who belongs to what caste?) does not arise here. Caste behavior is situational. Rules about ranking, occupation, subordination, and ritual relations come up, not abstractly, as a set of rules, but in situations. One's caste and its relation to other castes are always situational. Age, education, economic position, political connections, personality, and friendship also intervene and are taken into account. Nonetheless, it is possible to extract a description of how caste operates in the village context.

The hierarchy or ranking of *jatis* within a village and its local area is the most obvious characteristic of a local caste system. In a particular local system, the top and the bottom of the caste hierarchy are usually well known by all participants in the local system if Brahmans are part of the system. If Brahmans are the dominant landholding group, they are clearly the top caste in the system, because they have both the attributes of high ritual caste status, and economic and political power. In situations in which Brahmans are few and not significant holders of land, some anomalies arise. Brahmans are granted deference in ritual situations, but in the interactional context, their status is not so high as the dominant landholding caste. The highest caste in a summation of statuses for most purposes is the dominant landholding caste. In some areas these are Brahmans; in most areas other castes: Rajput, Gujar, Jat, Maratha, Okkaliga, Rddi Komti, Khandait, or even Muslim. Other castes tend to be ranked in relation to the dominant caste.

The relative positions of castes within the local ranking system can be seen symbolically acted out on ritual occasions when people attend feasts. The usual occasion for a feast is at the time of a life-cycle ceremony, that is, birth, marriage, death, or sometimes when a special ceremony has been performed in a household. Except on formal ritual occasions, there is little interdining among households or among members of the different *jatis* in a village. The normal hospitality pattern in an Indian village does not include the casual social exchange of meals among friends and neighbors. When different families and different castes eat together, it is a ritual occasion. Where one sits on such occasions, who cooks the food, when one is fed, with what, and by whom, symbolize the local caste ranking. The rules for dining and cooking are simple in principle. High status is symbolized by being able to take the rarest kinds of food from the fewest people. It is much better to give and have one's food taken than it is to receive. A Brahman theoretically can take only uncooked food from anyone of lower status than himself; hence, at a feast, a Brahman should cook his own food.

At a feast, people sit on mats in rows. The Brahman is by himself on his own mat, often cooking his own food. Other castes are graded down from the Brahman, with the untouchables hanging on the fringe, waiting for the leavings from the plates of the higher castes.

The landed dominant caste is at the center of a whole series of exchanges that can be seen as acting out relations. The dominant caste exchanges the right to use land for the labor and money of other castes. Not only do they exchange the use of land for money and labor, but they also gain followers in local political tussles as part of the exchange. In many areas of India, one establishes a tie to the person who "owns" the land on which one's house is built. In northern India this is called the *Thakur-Praja* tie (lord and follower). With those providing crafts, products, and services, the dominant caste person exchanges a share of the crop grown on his land or rights over land use for goods and services through an exchange system called the *jajmani* system. The *jajmani* system is not merely a means of distributing goods and services in exchange for grain and land, but has a ritual component as well.

Families within particular *jatis* provide services and goods to other families. In turn, they receive a fixed amount of grain and some goods. The services rendered are the carrying out of rituals by priests, water carrying, scavenging, carrying off refuse and dead animals, barbering, and washing clothes. The goods usually provided are plows and other implements as well as their maintenance and repair by carpenters or blacksmiths, provision of pottery vessels by the potter, and leaf plates by the leaf-plate maker. The kind and amount of goods and services rendered vary from place to place and from caste to caste. For example, a landholding dominant caste may have ten or twelve different families of other castes providing it with goods and services in the *jajmani* system, but a lower caste may have only two or three.

The exchange, though, is not just economic; there is always a ritual component to a relationship that is permanent and hereditary for both parties. Again the ties in the *jajmani* system binding families of different castes together can be seen at life-cycle rites, such as weddings, where much of the paraphernalia used must be made by one's *kamin* or *parjuniya* (the worker or giver of services). The carpenter provides the stand on which the bride-to-be washes herself and the birds that are part of the decoration of the shelter under which the wedding ceremony takes place. The barber must be present to provide certain services. The wife of the family Chamar leads the new bride on a tour of the sacred places of the village. In different villages and different regions, the services performed or the goods provided may vary, but the presence of the provider of the goods and services is necessary for the ceremony or ritual to be carried out.

There has been much argument about the question of how exploitative the *jajmani* system is, in that services and goods are rendered at a fixed or customarily fixed price, and payment made by landed elite groups is less than that made by other groups. Another set of questions related to the exploitation issue is whether fewer and fewer transactions are taking place within the customary exchange system as more and more goods are transferred on the open market. The issues are related, since if members of the dominant caste can maintain its hold over the *parjuniyas* or *kamins* and keep prices down to their customary level, they clearly stand to benefit at a time when prices of goods and services are rising. As with many questions about change and the rate of change in India, we must note that the empirical evidence is far from clear, given the lack of specific historical comparisons for particular villages.

Logically and empirically, it is clear that the number of transactions and the number of specialists involved in the *jajmani* system, in its narrowest sense, are declining because of technological change. For example, the introduction of the safety razor and its widespread use in the villages has reduced the number of times one is shaved by his barber. Conversely, the rise of "barber shops" in towns, on roadsides, and in bazaars has opened up a lucrative occupation for the barber. During the last fifty years, the potter has felt the increasing competition of cheap metal, china, and glass utensils and plates, and so today, except for large storage devices and pottery for ritual occasions, there is little demand for his services. The installation of hand pumps within houses has cut down on the need for water carriers and servants. Many of the traditional artisans would like to be free of the hereditary contractual tie, because they could market their skills and products more lucratively in the open market.

A more serious blow to the hereditary exchange system has been dealt by *zamindari* abolition. It is often overlooked that part of the payment in the system was a grant of land to the artisan or serving family, along with the regular payment of grain at the time of harvest. Most of the artisans and servants granted land under this system, at least in Uttar Pradesh, were classified as permanent or hereditary tenants; at *zamindari* abolition, they became in effect owners of their own land. Hence, many argued that since they were now their own landlords, their hereditary tie to their *jajmans* was broken. In those cases where the servant or artisan was a tenant-at-will, he tended to lose his land if the landlord had the land recorded in his own name. Hence, the dispossessed tenant felt that his obligation was ended. As discussed below, broad-scale economic and political changes have affected the village in the last two generations and, in a real sense, have tended to loosen the hold that the dominant caste traditionally had over other castes. Mutual interdependence and the division of labor involved in local caste systems have tended to be eroded, although with a concomitant strengthening of internal ties within the *jatis*.

CASTE AND SOCIAL MOBILITY

The strengthening of internal caste ties is most clear in the recent widespread attempt, throughout much of rural India, of *jatis* and *jats* to raise their status within the local caste system and to establish new customs and attributes that would lead to higher status in a wider society. Upward mobility in rural India tends to be a group phenomenon; although there is variation in individual status, the status of the *jati* to which one belongs in formal situations overrides variation in individual status.

In the village where I did field work, there are several primary school-teachers from the Chamar *jat*. One in particular, the son of an influential Chamar in the village, has done much to change his personal status. He wears clothes like those of a high-caste person, wears shoes, speaks *Kahri Boli*, the standard Hindi, is a vegetarian, and is knowledgeable about the world around him. Outside of the village, he is treated as a schoolteacher, a position held in respect, rather than as a Chamar. In his village where, of course, his caste status is known, he is referred to as the Chamar schoolteacher. He is addressed, as are low- and medium-caste teachers, by the title "munshi"; upper caste teachers are addressed by the English title "master." The ambiguity of his personal status is neatly symbolized by seating arrangements when he is at the house of a *Thakur* (landlord) in the village. Chamars squat on the ground when at the house of a landlord, but members of the landlord caste and some of the medium-rank castes sit or lie on the string cots. When the Chamar schoolteacher comes to a landlord's house, he is given a small stool or an overturned basket to sit on, thereby indicating that he is different from other Chamars but that his education and occupation are not suffi-cient to raise him to the *charpoy* (string bed). At his school, he does sit on a *charpoy* with the other teachers, but usually at the less honorific end of it.

Although anthropologists and others speak of mobility in the caste system, they are speaking not of individual mobility but of group mo-bility. Mobility within the caste system tends to begin with economic or political change. F. G. Bailey has documented how a very low caste in the Orrisan Hills, the Boad distillers, through their occupation as distillers and sellers of alcoholic beverages, the sale of which was en-couraged for tax purposes by the British in the nineteenth and early twentieth centuries, made substantial amounts of money with which they bought land and established themselves as a landed group. They were successful in raising their status. In changing their customs of eating and ritual observance, they came closer to the upper-class Sanskritic model and substantially raised their caste rank within the local system, becoming an important and powerful caste generally in the Orissan highlands.[4]

I have studied the attempt of a *jati* of Chamars in a village in eastern Uttar Pradesh to raise their status during a fifty-year period. At least three generations ago, the Chamars of Senapur, who were believed until that time to have eaten beef, stopped eating beef. The sanction today among the Senapur Chamars for eating beef is outcasting. When a person is outcasted, no one in his *biradari* will have social relations with him. He is literally barred from using wells and from smoking with his caste fellows. The ultimate sanction involved in outcasting is the prevention of marriage of the children of the family or man outcasted. The cessation of eating beef on the part of the Chamars was aimed at eliminating what was widely believed to be the most degraded custom of the Chamars: eating the flesh of the cow. At the same time, the Chamars stopped carting manure to the fields of the Thakurs and tried, ultimately unsuccessfully, to have the Chamar women stop making dung cakes for fuel for the Thakur households, because these were considered degrading activities. Sporadically since the period of the First World War, the Chamars have attempted to stop having to deal with dead animals. The attempt has been more on an individual than a corporate basis, and some Chamars have been successful in getting out of such work.

Along with the eschewing of customs or activities thought to be degrading, the Chamars evolved an ideology to account for their aspirations for upward mobility. The Chamar origin myths are much like the origin myths of most middle- and lower-rank castes. These myths involve a fall, usually through accident or the ill will of others, from a higher to a lower status. In the myth of the Chamars of Senapur, they claim to have been Brahmans or, in some versions, Rajputs, who by accident were responsible for the death of a cow and hence became untouchables. The Chamars' mythological hero is Raidas, a Bhakti saint of the sixteenth century. Raidas, a shoemaker, was recognized as saintly during his lifetime, although his caste status was low. Chamars in much of northern India call themselves Raidasis or by the name of particular Chamar *jatis* to avoid the denigrating term Chamar. Each year, the Chamars of Senapur and the surrounding area join in the celebration of Raidas's birthday, which today is increasingly taking on political overtones and is the

---

[4] F. G. Bailey, *Caste and the Economic Frontier* (Manchester: Manchester University Press, 1957).

occasion when new-style, politicized, younger, educated Chamars try to build followings among their rural caste brothers.

Another element in the Chamars' attempts to raise their status has been their participation in the Sivanarain religious sect. The ritual and theology of the sect are similar to orthodox Hindu practice. There are several major Sivanarain temples in cities such as Kanpur and Bombay and a loosely structured organization that, in the rural area, has leaders, called *mahants*, who hold regular meetings and rituals. It has become the Chamar version of orthodox Hinduism.

Thus far, in efforts at social mobility on the part of the Chamars from the period of the First World War until the 1930s, several things can be noted. The efforts can largely be subsumed under the term "Sanskritization," used by M. N. Srinivas and others to describe the process by which lower castes emulate the customs, values, and life style of higher castes in an attempt to raise their social status.[5] The concept of Sanskritization brings us to the fourth level of the caste system, the *varna* model. The caste system consists of four *varnas:* Brahman (priestly), Kshatriya (warrior), Vasiya (trader), and Shudra (worker or tiller); all castes except the untouchables are supposed to fit into one of these four large attributional cultural categories with diagnostic customs—the vegetarianism of the Brahman, for example. The cultural categories of the *varna* system provide general mobility models for upwardly aspiring castes. The *varna* model is useful in that aspiration is not toward a particular *jati*—which would be impossible, because it would entail intermarriage and great conflict—but toward claiming higher status generally without necessarily establishing new social relations with other *jatis.*[6]

Sanskritization is an affirmation, not a negation, of the caste system. Those groups who try to raise their status through Sanskritization are maintaining the caste system by accepting its values.

In the late 1930s, and increasingly in the forties and early fifties, Chamar efforts to raise their status shifted from the cultural to the economic and political arena. The first indication of a new kind of effort came dramatically just after the elections under the new constitution of 1935, late in 1936. Some Chamars of Senapur, although they themselves could not vote, supported a candidate not approved by the Thakurs and followed some of the leaders of the Noniya caste—a caste of agriculturalists and earth workers who themselves were involved in an attempt to claim Kshatriya status and were opposed by the Thakur landlords of

[5] See M. N. Srinivas, *Social Change in Modern India* (Berkeley and Los Angeles: University of California Press, 1966), Chap. 1.

[6] Owen M. Lynch, *The Politics of Untouchability* (New York: Columbia University Press, 1969).

the village. In punishment for this support, some Thakurs burned the houses of the Chamars involved and beat them. The Chamars previously would have knuckled under in the face of this aggression and would have begged forgiveness. This time, however, they left the village with their cattle and meagre belongings, went to the district headquarters, and sought help from the local Congress Committee and the intervention of the district government. Through legal maneuverings and their access to the lower levels of the bureaucracy, the Thakurs were able to blunt the Chamar threat to their authority; but, in a sense, having threatened legal and political action against the Thakurs, the Chamars were challenging the Thakurs' status in the village and developing a new identity for themselves.

With the increasing activity that led to Independence in 1947, the urban-based nationalist movement increasingly moved into the countryside and drew more and more small-town folk and village-based persons into the movement both as followers and leaders. In addition to the argument for freedom from the British, the ideology of social and economic equality was increasingly heard in the rural areas. This movement for equality reached a peak with the assassination of Gandhi in 1948, who, among other things, advocated fairer treatment of the untouchables. In many villages in India in 1948, including Senapur, a meal was held thirteen days after Gandhi's death, the traditional day for a mourning feast, at which different castes sat and ate together, symbolically affirming Gandhi's efforts to bring more freedom to the untouchables. Shortly after this, local elections were to be held to establish a democratically elected village council; all adults were to be able to vote in this election. The lower castes in the village, including the Chamars, organized to contest this election and put up a slate of candidates who opposed the dominant Thakur-selected candidates. The party formed was called the *nicé kaum,* "the party of the lowers." They were successful in getting their slate elected, but because they had no source of informal power in the village, the economic hold of the Thakurs continued unabated. The lower castes were unable to make the village council function to their advantage. At this time, the Chamars not only had political goals but also began a strike for higher wages. This proved unsuccessful, and their leaders, with some leaders of the lower-caste party, were punished and beaten; one of them actually was killed. In the early 1950s when I was doing field work, most Chamars had lost heart in their attempt to better their political and economic status. Other changes, such as those attendant on Zamindari abolition (land reform), which is discussed below, have increasingly become intertwined with attempts of groups like the Chamars and higher-ranking castes to raise their status.

Owen Lynch's detailed and fascinating study of the Chamars, called *The Politics of Untouchability,* indicates the likely direction of changes within the caste system and the strategies increasingly followed by lower castes to achieve a fairer share of the valued statuses and goods of Indian society.[7]

Agra is an old city whose earliest history and origin are lost in myth and legend. Its modern rise dates from the sixteenth century, and from then until the eighteenth century Agra shared prominence with Delhi as a major center of Mughal authority. Under the British for a time in the early nineteenth century, it was an important political center. From the middle of the nineteenth century to the present, it has had the status of an important provincial center, though not the significance in Uttar Pradesh of Kanpur, the major industrial center, Lucknow, the capital, or Banaras, the great shrine center. Nonetheless, it has important educational and cultural institutions and is a commercial center for western Uttar Pradesh and adjacent parts of Rajasthan and Madhya Pradesh.

The Jatavs of today date their residence in Agra from the middle of the nineteenth century, when several of the *mohallas* (wards) of the city were Chamar *mohallas.* In 1961 there were more than 71,000 Chamars in Agra, almost all of whom were Jatavs. The Chamars are about one-sixth of the nearly 500,000 persons in Agra city.[8]

Although there were many continuities from the village into the city, both in structure and culture, the sheer numbers involved in a city led to major differences between the life lived by the Chamars in Agra and that of the Chamars in a village like Senapur. The most obvious change, which for the Jatavs dates back to the late nineteenth century, was the introduction of new kinds of internal differentiation within the *jati.* The Chamars had a traditional form of organization based on their *mohallas,* which could be likened to villages where large numbers of Chamars lived somewhat self-contained lives. *Mohallas* had headmen, were governed by well-organized panchayats, and practised *mohalla* exogamy. The traditional social and political structure was not unlike that found among Chamars of larger villages. The differences began to appear as members' success in the economic sphere varied. A few Chamars began to get rich through different forms of contracting and building activities. After the 1920s, when the Chamars began to concentrate heavily on their traditional occupation of shoemaking, the differentiation became even greater. Some Chamars became quite successful as organizers of craftlike factories for the production of shoes and sandals.

---

[7] *Ibid.*
[8] *Ibid.,* p. 31.

At the time of the First World War, through the schools opened by the Arya Samaj, a Hindu reform movement, some Chamars began to get an education.

The more successful and richer Chamars took advantage of the Arya Samaj schools as well as the schools of the missionaries and the government. The presence of a wealthy and educated group of Jatavs brought forth a new kind of leader among them called the *barre admi*, the "big men." In the 1920s the "big men" wholeheartedly began a campaign of Sanskritization, complete with published texts giving Jatav mythological histories and justifying their claims to Kshatriya status; formal organizations were set up to spread propaganda for this purpose and to defend the Jatavs' interests with the government. The phase of social mobility through Sanskritization and acceptance of the caste system continued into the 1930s. During the 1920s and 1930s, the Jatavs in Agra began to have the direct experience of "petitional politics," which were in accordance with the efforts of the British government in India to introduce slowly recognized institutions of self-government. At the time, this meant counsel and advice to the administration by those being ruled rather than much direct power and authority over government. Nonetheless, the participation of some of the "big men" in politics "by petition" in the municipal and district boards was important to the self-esteem of the Jatavs, since it allowed them to act as other caste groups were acting at that period. Most upper castes also had "their" representatives involved in these "self"-governing institutions.

In the 1930s, with the intensification of the nationalist movement and the speedup of British attempts to find a constitutional solution for the demands of self-rule and independence, a series of high-level conferences were held, at which communities, as defined by the British, and interests, such as the princes and the British commercial groups, were represented. The Jatavs of Agra were now participating fully in petitional politics as a group and as individuals, as members of their caste with the requisite increasing education were elected or appointed to administrative service posts to act as spokesmen and leaders. Until the late 1930s, there did not seem to be any conflict between the efforts at Sanskritization and raising the cultural status of the Jatavs of Agra, and their participation in the petitional politics of the time. In fact, the two activities reinforced each other. With the obvious increasing success of the Congress-led nationalist movement, by the end of the 1930s, the British faced the question, not of whether to grant self-rule or independence, but of when to grant it. The Jatavs, however, began to perceive a new set of difficulties. By and large, they defined the Congress movement as a caste Hindu movement, particularly a Brahman-led movement; it was the

Brahmans, the Jatavs believed, who were responsible for their degraded traditional position.

This led to an about-face in the strategies of mobility and identification. The Jatavs now began wholehearted identification with the Scheduled Caste Federation led by B. R. Ambedkar, the Maharashtrian leader of the Majars who was developing a movement to free all Untouchables from the grave disabilities under which they were forced to live. Identification with Ambedkar and the Scheduled Caste Federation, in fact, meant a strategy not of group mobility that affirmed the values of the caste system, but a rejection of the system and a joining in the battle for abolishing it. The Jatavs joined a movement whose goals became the abolition of all discrimination, in the form of prohibition of temple entry, use of public and some private facilities, such as restaurants, and exclusion from certain jobs. According to law, this fight has been successful. Each state has anti-Untouchable discrimination laws in its books, and the Constitution adopted in 1950 outlaws all forms of caste discrimination. In practice, however, many of the disabilities and discriminatory practices continued.

In the 1950s and 1960s, the Jatavs of Agra turned in two directions in their fight for equality: to politics and to conversion to Buddhism. Having taken over the opposition party in municipal affairs during the sixties, the Jatavs are trying to gain more advances through their political power. Through their conversion to Buddhism, they have culturally withdrawn, they feel, from Hindu society and no longer consider themselves held by the bonds of the caste system. The conversion to Buddhism was part of a movement started by Ambedkar to have untouchables secede from Hindu society, because it was not affecting changes in practice and attitude that the Untouchables, particularly in western India, believed were necessary.

The Jatav experience and strategies as described and analyzed by Lynch indicate, I think, directions that Untouchables, such as the Chamars of Senapur, are likely to take. The vote has been a powerful symbolic factor, even for illiterate rural Chamars, in their struggle for upward mobility. In national and local elections now, even in a village like Senapur, the caste Hindus, the representatives of the dominant caste, must come into the Chamar hamlets to seek votes if there is any split among the dominant group; and usually there is such a split. The leaders of the dominant groups must compete with one another for votes to get their candidates elected. The Chamar and other low social and economic groups now have something the dominant groups want other than merely their labor, namely, their votes.

In the cultural realm, conversion to Buddhism means the adoption of an ideology that is nonhierarchic. By becoming a Buddhist, one is not trying to raise one's caste status, but is identifying with a noncaste ideology.

SUMMARY

In the last 100 years there has been extensive change in the Indian caste system. The rate of change has increased, particularly in the last 30 years. The basic change has been to strengthen and extend the internal bonds within *jats* and to begin to make the *jats* more than just a cultural category. Marriage networks have expanded, and so older rules concerning marriage within the *jatis* have been relaxed, particularly for upper castes; and marriage now tends to cut across *jati* lines in a way that was not possible several generations ago. The endogamous unit is becoming the *jat*. Caste is one way by which groups enter the modern electoral political arena, although it is by no means the only one. The working of the system is making attributional features more important than interactional ones, particularly in the urban setting, where individuals and groups in a range of situations increasingly interact on other than caste principles but where the attributes of different castes are still used for identification and broad groupings of social behavior.

Public ideology, as represented by the Constitution, has set forward a goal of equality for society, and theoretically, although not actually, the weight of the administrative and judicial system can be applied to this end. Democratic politics has caused new groupings and interests to be put ahead of narrowly defined local caste interests, and although leaders bemoan what they term "castism," putting one's caste ahead of other interests is itself something new.

There is an increasing number of situations in which one's caste is of little importance, particularly in the modern economy, where roles tend to be achieved rather than ascribed. Discrimination and prejudice are used as terms in the newspapers and by educated Indians to describe attitudes and behavior in which people are disadvantaged by their caste ascription. That concepts such as discrimination and prejudice are becoming widespread and applied to many practices taken as normal or expected just a few generations ago indicates that the system is rapidly changing.

In the rural areas the situation is changing also, particularly in response to broad-scale political changes, the spreading of new official ideologies, and basic economic changes affecting the agricultural segment of society.

CHAPTER TWELVE

The Indian Village

In 1961, 360 million of India's 439 million persons were classified as rural by the Indian census. These 360 million, or 82 percent of the population, lived in some 567,000 villages. For census and administrative purposes, a village is defined arbitrarily and does not necessarily coincide with sociological reality. The sociological reality may be defined as what people conceive of as "their" village. The most obvious way to define villages in India is to consider their settlement pattern, which varies widely from place to place according to the geography, the kind of agriculture practiced, and the tradition and history of the area in which the village is located.

It is useful to consider three kinds of settlement patterns of Indian villages: the nucleated, the hamleted, and the dispersed. A *nucleated* village pattern is one with houses quite close together in a defined village site, sometimes walled, with narrow lanes and with the fields of the village spread around the settlement site. Such villages are typical of western Uttar Pradesh, Delhi, the Punjab, and some parts of southern India. Statistically, the *hamleted* village is probably more typical and tends to be found in most of the middle and lower Ganges and parts of Tamilnad and Andhra. In this pattern, there is usually a central settlement, several hamlets, and satellite settlements scattered over the fields of the village. A *dispersed* pattern is found in many shifting deltic areas, such as the mouths of the Ganges in lower Bengal, on the Kerala coast, at the southern tip of India, and in many of the hill regions in the northern and central highlands. There is no obvious village, because homesteads are dispersed, generally on or near the fields owned or worked on by the agriculturalists. One cannot tell from observation, as one can with the nucleated or hamleted village, where one village begins and another ends. Except in the hills, the dispersed village is associated with rice production, the hamleted village with a mixed rice and other grain agriculture, and the nucleated usually with wheat, barley, and millet production and with dry farming.

The size of a village's population is another means of classification, because size tends to be correlated with the nature of caste composition in the village and the pattern of political dominance. The three variables of size, caste composition, and political structure may be handled together. I am following the classification developed by the anthropologist, Alan Beals.[1]

The three kinds of villages are (1) villages with a small population of a single caste, (2) small multicaste villages with a single head, and (3) multicaste villages with a dominant caste resident.

Villages with a Small Population of a Single Caste

In Beal's classification, these villages are found in particular ecological niches, usually with a specialized economy, such as herding, fishing, or craft production. The bounds of such a village are also the bounds of the *biradari*. Politics center on both *biradari* and village affairs. Such villages tend to be governed by councils that enforce caste rules and adjudicate other disputes arising from the day-to-day affairs of the village. The norms of the caste and the village are well known to everyone, and "public opinion," as directed by the council, is the most effective means of social control.

Small Multicaste Villages with a Single Head

In some smaller villages with a number of castes, through governmental action or a single household's success during several generations in controlling a significant part of the land, one person, in his office as headman or in his role as the head of the most powerful and richest household, is in effect the head of the village. Dube describes such a headman, the Deshmukh of Shamirpet, a village in Mysore near Hyderabad City:

By virtue of his wealth, position and the contacts he maintains with powerful government officials, the Deshmukh is a pivotal figure in the village and

---

[1] "Cleavage and Internal Conflict: An Example from India," *The Journal of Conflict Resolution*, 5 (1961), 27–34; *Gopalpur: A South Indian Village* (New York: Holt, Rinehart & Winston, 1962), pp. 84–89; and "Conflict and Interlocal Festivals in a South Indian Region," *Journal of Asian Studies*, 23 (1964), 99–113.

enjoys a position of great influence. Although his word is no longer law, he still wields very great influence in the village and is always given a place of honour at all village ceremonies. Village disputes of any importance are always referred to him, and his decisions are seldom disregarded.[2]

Single-head villages are found in most parts of India. In areas such as Uttar Pradesh and Bihar, where there were large landlords—sometimes owning several or dozens of villages—and in the south, where the British government appointed and made hereditary the office of village headman, they are more prevalent. The tendency in the north, with the presence of lineages as landholding bodies, is for official headship as an office to be held by a number of men. In Maharashtra, the village office of headman could be sold or inherited in fractional parts; the office was economically valuable, since the headman received certain tax benefits and was paid a small percentage of the land revenue collected through his efforts. In many parts of India, land reform has turned what had been single-head villages into multicaste and dominant-caste villages. Kishan Garhi, a village in western Uttar Pradesh, described by McKim Marriott, before 1910, had a single Brahman landlord. There are now several landed castes competing for power in the village.[3] A village in eastern Uttar Pradesh, studied by Harold Gould, which had had a single important family of Rajputs as the dominant head, now has, since the loss of some of the headman's landed rights, the medium-rank Ahir caste as the important caste in the village. They now hold most of the land and have supplanted the former landlord family as the dominant group in the village.[4]

Multicaste Villages with the Dominant Caste Resident

The model of structure most common in anthropological literature on village India is of a village with 800 to 2,000 people, ten to twenty castes, and one landholding caste, such as Rajput, Jat Okkaliga, or Brahman, dominant both politically and economically. In such a village, the dominant caste generally does not exercise its political and economic dominance corporately, but each of its significant households controls families of other castes in a variety of ways. We have discussed the *jajmani* system, in which a landholding family is at the center of the system of distribution of goods and services, at customary rates, with some ritual

---

[2] S. C. Dube, *Indian Village* (Ithaca, N.Y.: Cornell University Press, 1955), p. 65.
[3] McKim Marriott, "Social Structure and Change in an Uttar Pradesh Village," in *India's Villages* (Calcutta: West Bengal Government Press, 1955).
[4] Harold Gould, "The Incident of the Fish," in Robert Sakai (ed.), *Studies on Asia, 1963* (Lincoln, Nebraska: University of Nebraska Press).

interdependence. Even more important for the political structure of the village is the tie between "lord" and "follower." This may be formally recognized, as it is in the *Thakur-Praja* relationship found in Uttar Pradesh, where a follower builds his house on the land "owned" by his Thakar (lord). The relationship of the land controller to the actual cultivators of the soil has a wide range of legal definitions, which has confused the understanding of internal village structure in India. In functional terms, the actual legal definition of the rights that various parties hold over land in the village context matters little. But it can usually be seen in the multicaste village, with resident dominant caste families or even a single dominant head, that one family has control over the use of the land and another pays for the right to cultivate the land in the form of money, in kind, or in services or labor. According to law, both parties may be defined as "tenants" or were so defined before land reform. But in the exercise of political control, the power to get someone to do what you want, one tenant may be dominant.

The power that a dominant caste has as a corporate group in a village or group of villages is potential, because power rests, not with the caste, but with individuals and families in the caste. In fact, more conflict in the multicaste dominant-caste village occurs within the dominant caste than across caste lines or in the exercise of direct power by one caste over others. The families of the dominant caste usually compete with one another for power, land, and social status. Power is directly correlated with land control, and one can sometimes attract followers from the poorer families of the dominant caste as well as from the lower castes. Ultimately, although many other factors influence it, power and authority in the Indian village rests on the effective use of force, symbolized by the ability to call out one's followers, armed with *lathis* (a stout bamboo staff), to fight with other groups.

The competition within the dominant caste for control of resources and people leads to a situation in which there are factions in the village. A faction may be defined, in the Indian context, as a series of alliances across caste lines, frequently shifting in their nature and organized or maintained by one or several families of the dominant caste as a means of gaining control of the village.

Analyzing factions in the Indian context has proved difficult. Factions, competition, violence, and single-minded pursuit of the goals of self and family interest are at odds with the expressed public ideology of leadership and politics, which puts wisdom rather than force at the center of Indian political values. It considers negation of material ends a prime goal, values the role of wise arbitrator rather than victor, and has the religiously based value of self-control as central. In the minds of many villagers, there is clearly a conflict between what they really think is right—the furthering of their own ends—and public ideology.[5]

Given the conflict between public ideology and the severe struggle, many villagers are unwilling to discuss the situation with outsiders. As the organization of factions tends to shift in time, situations, and contingencies, there is frequent confusion as to who is in which faction at what time. For tactical reasons, many try to keep secret their allegiances to one or another faction and its leaders. The number of factions can vary from time to time; two is the usual number, but at times there may be more.

In spite of all the possible combinations and the uncertainties of membership, a model of a faction system in a village can be described. The factional system of a village begins with the opposition of two individuals or families, usually members of the same *biradari* or *jati*, who are competing for status and power. Status within a *biradari* or even within a *jati* is not perfectly ordered, as theoretically it can be within a local caste system. Within a *biradari*, constantly shifting family fortunes, in terms of property control, the personalities and experience of individuals, and the demography, in a short-term sense, give one family many adult males at one time and another only a few. A wide range of minutely differing situations in which a family or an individual wants support is possible. A family with one adult male with considerable land needs followers to balance a less well-off family with many sons or close agnatic kin as a ready source of manpower. In order to get the manpower needed, the richer, single individual establishes alliances by offering help, giving advice, loaning money, and promising support to others in their disputes. Initially the faction is based on a few alliances within the dominant caste and then branches out for manpower into other castes.

In the Indian village context, the possibility of dispute is very great, and many disputes are among agnatic kin in the same *biradari*. The inheritance system divides property equally among brothers. When a joint household of several brothers does partition its property, feeling about unfair dealings may run high. Land, especially when it is greatly subdivided, cannot be shared exactly. Ownership of cattle and of facilities such as wells, sheds, and bullock carts can be the cause of acrimonious dispute. The vagaries of mortality—leaving a minor male as head of a household or a widow in charge of property on a temporary basis—can

---

[5] On "traditional" political values, see Myron Weiner, "Struggle Against Power: Notes on Indian Political Behavior," *World Politics*, 8 (1956), 392–403, and Susanne H. Rudolph, "Consensus and Conflict in Indian Politics," *World Politics*, 13 (1961), 385–99. For a psychoanalytical discussion of the conflict between "traditional" political values and reality of the situation in which most Indian villages find themselves, see Morris Carstairs, *The Twice Born* (London: Hogarth, 1957).

also lead to disputes. Once started, disputes can go through several generations, the kin getting more and more genealogically separated but maintaining what is almost a permanent relationship of conflict.

In the lower castes, sources of dispute among kin also include accusations of sexual misconduct and cheating a caste fellow out of land; property disputes across caste lines arise over grazing of cattle, crop stealing, encroachment on land, and arguments over the use of facilities such as wells. At a particular time in a village, there are innumerable squabbles, going on obviously or just below the surface, many of which can be transferred to the arena of faction politics.

In recent years, elections to village office have added another source of dispute, as have the distribution of government grants, the building of schools and public facilities, the placement of tube wells, the digging of irrigation channels, and the building of roads. Any situation that obliges an individual or group to part with property can be a source of conflict.

The operation of factions, although sometimes negative in effect, can be positive in encouraging groups to cooperate across caste lines. Not all activities in the village are organized along factional lines. Ceremonial occasions cut across factions; often villages organize fairs or festivals irrespective of factions, and when there is agreement about the need for a village structure, such as a school, differing groups organize to obtain it. Finally, the factional system diffuses power. As soon as one faction or factional leader seems on the verge of defeating his opponents, his own faction often splits, because some of his followers fear that too much power is concentrated in one leader.

Recent Changes in Village Structure

Structurally, a paradox is developing in the relationship of Indian villages to the wider society. It was stated earlier that the village, as we have known it in the last 200 years or so, is partially a function of the conditions of British rule. In the eighteenth century, the basic unit of local social structure was not the village, but a collection of villages forming the "little kingdom," the territory of a local chief or raja, or a complex centered on a temple or a lineage. With the political and revenue system introduced by the British, particularly in relation to land tenure, the village has increasingly become the center of local politics. The strengthening of the village as a local unit can be seen in the effects of tenure legislation during the last 100 years, which, in northern India, always led to concentrating the lands and interests of land-controlling groups into smaller and smaller locations. Zamindari abolition, or the elimination of what were thought to be the "big landlords" in the early

1950s, caused landlords to lose what lands they held in other areas and tied them to a single village. Among some relatively powerful land-holders, who had shares in several villages, the alternative was to establish sons or grandsons and their families in other villages than those in which the heads of household had their houses. Formerly, all the sons or agnatic cousins in such a household would live in one house and supervise their lands from one center. Now, in order to hold land in other villages, they had to seem residents, not absentee landlords. Hence, they established residences in villages that formerly they had only visited. In a generation or two, the branches of families thus dispersed will become rooted in their new villages; and although kinship ties will be recognized in their home villages, they will become part of the villages they have moved to. There will still be "absentee" landlords—families with diversified interests based in towns and bazaars—who will be money-lenders, shopkeepers, or small-scale industrialists and landlords, but they will not be landlords owning thousands of acres as we have found until the early 1950s.

As we discussed earlier, the present situation will probably continue for some time; that is, there will be a class of moderately powerful land-lords, or substantial peasants, none of whom will dominate large numbers of villages. These men will be connected with the political parties and related to the lower and middle levels of the local and district administrations. They will continue to benefit, in their agricultural activities, from the efforts of the government to modernize and improve Indian agriculture. The substantial peasants have the contacts, and they have or will have the education, land, capital, and resources to improve their agricultural production. They have the economic margin to risk investing in new seeds and new productive techniques. As Indian agriculture improves, they will be the main beneficiaries, thereby consolidating their positions of dominance in their villages. But the villages they will dominate are changing from those we have known during the last 100 years or so. The villages are becoming more like the peasant villages of Europe, with fairly broad strata of peasant proprietors producing for the market, with a few tenants and hired help. In recent years, land reform in many areas has enlarged the pool of landless citizens who are drifting to the cities or who will become increasingly involved in rural services that are not part of the village economy; motorized transportation, construction, part-time work in local food processing of grain, rice, and sugar, and small-scale production of other rural necessities, such as brick and tiles. Increasingly, the artisans will produce for markets rather than for exchange within the village, although they may be residents in villages, serving as agriculturalists. As at no other time in the history of India, the local, state, and central governments have penetrated directly into the villages. This occurred first through the extraordinary expansion of primary schools since Independence, then through the proliferation of agricultural services, and finally through the development of electoral machinery for national and local elections. The influence of the government is sporadic and shallow, but it is there.

CITY INDIA

In 1961, almost 80 million Indians, or 18 percent of the population, lived in 2,700 places classified as towns and cities. In 1901, the percentage of the population counted as urban was a little under 11 percent. There was a spurt in the rate of urbanization in the period 1931 to 1951—from 12 to 17 percent. This was also a period of rapidly accelerating population growth, and so the absolute figures of 33 million urban in 1931 and 79 million urban in 1961 give a better idea òf the growth of cities during this period.

The rate of urbanization in the ten-year period from 1951 to 1961 was about 1 percent, although one student of urbanization in India, Ashish Bose, has argued that because of definitional adjustments and more accurate counting, by the criteria used in 1951, the growth in the 1951 to 1961 period was really closer to 2 percent.[6] Important and interesting variations within regions in terms of the degree of urbanization can be seen in Table 10.

For census purposes, the definition of *urban* has varied in time, and there are some variations even within a given year, by state. But as with most census definitions, that for towns and cities is largely based on administrative features, that is, the kind of administrative regulations the place is under and some consideration of size. But size clearly is not the only criterion used for defining urban population; more than 4,000 villages with a population of more than 5,000 account for 34 million persons or slightly less than 10 percent of the rural population.

Table 11 gives the number of persons living in towns and cities, by size. It is important to note that about 45 percent of the urban population lives in towns and cities of more than 100,000 persons.

We do not know as much in a quantitative sense as we should like to about the characteristics of India's urban population, but some important differences are known in a gross sense about urban populations as distinguished from rural populations. Among the more important characteristics of urban and rural populations are the following. There are more

[6] Ashish Bose, "Six Decades of Urbanization in India: 1901–1961," *The India Economic and Social History Review,* vol. 2, 1965, pp. 23–41.

TABLE 10

Order of percentage of the population living in urban areas, 1961

State	Percentage urban
1. Maharashtra	28.22
2. Madras	26.68
3. Gujarat	25.79
4. West Bengal	24.45
5. Mysore	22.34
6. Punjab	20.14
7. Andhra Pradesh	17.43
8. Jammu and Kashmir	16.57
9. Rajasthan	16.27
10. Kerala	15.09
11. Madhya Pradesh	14.30
12. Uttar Pradesh	12.85
13. Bihar	8.42
14. Assam	7.67
15. Orissa	6.32

SOURCE: Ashish Bose, "Six Decades of Urbanization in India: 1901–1961," *The India Economic and Social History Review*, 2 (1965), 32.

TABLE 11

Distribution of urban population by size of city

Size of City	Population in Millions
Over 100,000	35.1
50,000–99,999	9.5
20,000–49,999	15.8
10,000–19,999	11.3
Below 9,999	7.2
	78.9

SOURCE: Government of India, The Central Gazetteers Unit, The Gazetteer of India: Indian Union, Vol. I, "Country and People" (New Delhi: Publications Division, Ministry of Information and Broadcasting, 1965), p. 335.

males than females living in cities, with 116 males for every 100 females. This, of course, reflects the often observed pattern of urban migration, in which males migrate for a shorter or longer time to the cities for employment, leaving their wives and children behind. India's minority religious groups tend to be more urban than the Hindus.

The regional distribution of the various religious minorities (Table 12)

TABLE 12

Distribution of urban population by religion

Religion	Percentage urban
Parsi	95
Jain	54
Muslim	27
Christian	24
Sikhs	23
Hindu	16

explains their having a significant impact on the style of urban life in particular cities and regions. Although the Jains and Parsis are a small percentage of the population in Gujarat and Maharashtra, they are so highly urbanized that they are important social and economic groups in the cities
of Maharashtra and Gujarat. Most significant in terms of urbanization
are the Muslims, in both northern and southern India.

As can be seen from Table 13, in those states with a significant number
of Muslims, there are two patterns of Muslim urbanization. In eastern
India (Bengal, Bihar, and Assam), fewer Muslims live in cities than in
other states where they are a significant minority. In eastern India, the

TABLE 13

*Distribution of Muslim population in India in states
with more than 1 million Muslims*

State	Percentage of total population Muslim	Number of Muslims, 000 omitted	Percentage of total population urban	Percentage of Muslim population urban	Percentage of urban Muslim to total urban population
Assam	23.3	2,765	7.7	4.1	12.0
West Bengal	20.0	6,985	24.5	14.1	11.6
Kerala	17.9	3,027	15.1	17.4	20.3
Uttar Pradesh	14.6	10,788	12.9	25.6	29.5
Bihar	12.5	5,785	8.4	11.9	17.7
Mysore	9.9	2,328	22.3	43.5	18.9
Gujarat	8.5	1,745	25.8	51.8	17.0
Maharashtra	7.7	3,034	28.2	55.1	15.4
Andhra	7.5	2,715	17.4	44.8	19.0
Rajasthan	6.5	1,314	16.2	39.4	15.8
Madras	4.6	1,560	26.7	57.7	10.0
Madhya Pradesh	4.0	1,317	14.3	53.7	15.4

Muslims are more involved in agriculture as small proprietors and agricultural workers than they are in the rest of India.

The presence of Muslims in the cities is a reflection of the 800 years of Islamic rule over many parts of India. The pattern of Muslim rule, as discussed above, was to control the countryside from the towns, cities, and forts. The present-day Muslim population, then, reflects an older political tradition as well as the fact that many urban Muslims were craftsmen, often concentrated in the old political centers. The distribution of Muslims also is important to the recent political history of India, in that an urbanized population, with the exception of eastern India, makes the rapid organization of the Muslim League in the 1930s more understandable. It was easier to mobilize urban people, who were more concentrated than the peasants and more easily reached through mass media and political meetings as well as through traditional means of communication.

Early in the twentieth century, it was widely held that the Muslims lagged far behind the Hindus in accepting Western education. This is true in terms of the aggregate statistics, which include the rural Muslim population of eastern India, but in Uttar Pradesh, western and southern India, the Muslims, by the twentieth century, were well represented in the colleges and universities, and Muslim literacy rates were as high as those of their Hindu countrymen. But the Muslims, since they had for centuries lived an urban life, did not necessarily change their life style in the cities of the late nineteenth and twentieth centuries in the way some Hindu groups did. Often, the Muslim craftsmen and particularly the literati continued to live a traditional rather than a modern urban life.

There is a significant difference between the caste categories found in the cities and those in the rural areas. In the mid-fifties, 17 percent of the population of the cities and towns was drawn from the upper castes (Brahman, Rajput and similar groups, and the commercial castes), but these same castes accounted for only about 9 percent of the rural population. In cities of more than 50,000, the upper castes accounted for almost one-quarter of the population. The scheduled castes, who accounted for about 23 percent of the rural Hindu population, accounted for only 14 percent of the urban population.[7] The facts reflect two things about the sociology of both the traditional and the modern segments of Indian cities. In the past, it was the upper castes who were merchants, priests, literati, land controllers, and officials in the towns. Members of these upper castes, in the nineteenth and twentieth centuries,

[7] N. V. Sovani, "The Urban Social Situation in India," *Artha Vijnana*, 3 (1961), 88.

entered the Western-style schools and universities and obtained the training necessary for success in the new occupational structure which developed in the cities of India during the last 100 years and which is still expanding.

Contrary to general expectations about the effect of urbanization on family size, based on the experience of the West, where the urban family is usually smaller than the rural family, in India, although the urban family is somewhat smaller than the rural family, it is not markedly so. The all-India average is 5.03 persons per rural household and 4.59 per urban household. In the countryside, 24 percent of the population lives in households with seven or more members; in the cities, 21 percent of the population lives in such households. The size of the city is not significant in terms of the distribution of large households.

There is good reason to accept the fact that urbanization has not greatly affected the structure of the Indian family.[8] As would be expected, a significant statistical difference between rural and urban populations in India relates to the question of literacy and education, with almost half of the urban males literate, compared with 17 percent of the rural males. Slightly less than 1 percent of rural males have had the equivalent of a high school education; 9 percent of urban males have such an educational level.[9]

URBAN CULTURES

As has been suggested in this essay, a simple, Western-oriented view of urban life styles and the process of urbanization does not adequately explain the situation found in Indian cities today. The Indian city and town are both the center of traditional culture and the Indian variant of modern culture. A simple functional classification of Indian culture views cities such as Banaras or Hardwar as traditional, since they are centers of Hinduism, and Calcutta and Bombay as modern, since they were founded by the Europeans and are modern industrial and commercial centers. But this classification misses the reality of the situation. Nor can individuals in the cities be simply classified, on the basis of occupation or education, into participants in modern urban or traditional urban cultures.

Milton Singer, in studying managers and owners of large-scale industrial enterprises in Madras, a population in which Brahmans predominated, found that there was not necessarily a conflict between traditional southern Indian Brahmanical values—participation in ritual activities

[8] *Ibid.*, p. 89.
[9] *Ibid.*, p. 91.

and living in a joint family—and success in highly competitive, large-scale technological industry. The managers living in a traditional culture found no conflict between this and their participation in the modern industrial segment of society.[10]

Westerners frequently express amazement when they realize that a man with an advanced degree from a British or American university, who is the counterpart of the head of an engineering section of a large American firm or a higher civil servant in the government, who is completely at home in the English language and is familiar with the latest intellectual and political developments in the West, still lives in a traditional household. Westerners think that there is necessarily a conflict between the two worlds in which such a person lives. Both theoretically, as social scientists, and as individuals in our culture, we tend to look for role consistency in various situations. In the Indian context, one's whole socialization leads one to be very adept at playing different roles in different situations without any apparent conflict from one to another. In growing up in an Indian household, a male learns to be subservient to his father and, at the same time, to dominate his younger brother and the servants in the household. He learns that there can be a wide variety of life styles even in his own household and expects to find in society great differences in custom based on caste, religion, and economic status. So situations and behaviors that seem conflicting to us, who have grown up in a homogeneous culture and who expect relative consistency of behavior from those around us, do not cause any particular feeling of disjunction among Indians.

Shils has pointed out that Indians are socialized by females in the household—mothers, grandmothers, or servants who very often are illiterate and not at all exposed to Western or modern culture, as are the men of the household.[11] Their first world view, then, encompasses the traditional. Their acceptance of and orientation to modern cultures is learned later in life and, to some extent, as an intellectual exercise. The "modern" Indian is not a rootless person; he is firmly anchored in his traditional society and culture.

The rootedness derived from growing up in a traditional household may begin to change, however, as more and more middle-class Indian girls in the cities become educated and have experience outside of their homes or, as in the last few decades, they follow their husbands overseas

[10] Milton Singer, "The Indian Joint Family in Modern Industry," in Milton Singer and Bernard S. Cohn (eds.), *Structure and Change in Indian Society* (Chicago, 1968), pp. 423–52.

[11] Edward Shils, *The Intellectual between Tradition and Modernity: The Indian Situation* (The Hague: Moulton, 1961).

for education or to be with them while they are educated. More Indian women are postponing marriage in order to finish their education. When these highly educated Indian women establish households of their own and raise their own children, tradition may not be so strong in their households as it was when only the males were educated and exposed to modern values.

THE RELATIONSHIP OF VILLAGE TO CITY

It has been a persistent argument of this essay that, in time, there has been a typical relationship between city and village in Indian civilization, that the two are organically linked by networks of direct relationship structurally and by a common culture and a communications network.

Because of the structural changes that have taken place in rural Indian society during the last 100 years, the nature of the relationship between city and village is undergoing a change. The expansion of the administrative system in India, representation of the whole Indian population through elected bodies at the district, state, and national levels, and the commitment of the Indian government during the last twenty years to social welfare and economic development for the whole society have expanded the integration of the villager into the state and even the national levels. On the other hand, cultural integration seems to have changed considerably. The urban cosmopolitan model, with its orientation toward modern values, is not so directly connected with the countryside as the older Sanskritic or royal models, with their linked hierarchy of centers from the great religious or court centers. One enters the cosmopolitan modern culture by leaving the countryside, becoming educated, entering occupations far removed from the crafts and agriculture practised in the villages. For several generations, the social tie with one's home village may continue. The educated urban dweller, whether romantically or for more genuine reasons, appreciates and admires some of the virtues of his country relatives, but a gap is widening. The culture of the villages is more approximately a peasant culture in that, since land reform, the limitations on landed resources, and the virtual elimination of the large landholder, the cultural model of the landlord, formerly available for the emulation of smaller landholders and peasants, is rarely found in rural areas or in the towns and cities. The cultural gap between town and country, therefore, may be increasing.

The gap appears not only in the upper strata of society, economically and socially, but in the lower strata as well. Lower castes or the less well-educated upper-caste men move into the city and increasingly resemble the urban proletariat of Europe. They may organize differently and their goals may be different, but the conditions of the modern urban industrial environment are pushing the lower occupational ranks of the industrial sector into unions and political activity that will further their economic interests.

The rapid expansion of higher-education facilities is also widening the gap between town and country. Higher education in India is becoming less elitist in its acceptance of students. But although an increasing number of students come to the expanded older universities or the recently established new universities and colleges, in an overwhelming sense, they tend to remain in the urban setting, because the jobs they aspire to are there. The presence of the city, therefore, does not necessarily guarantee the effective diffusion of new values and behaviors into the countryside.

I have tried to indicate throughout that Indian society and culture, as in the past, are changing today, and that the nature and rate of change are governed by a wide range of factors.

Conclusion

In this essay there has been a constant effort to relate the past to the present and the present to the past. Continuity and change have been constant in the history of Indian civilization. What of the future of India? Is it possible that as a society and as a culture India can be radically transformed, such as Western society was transformed in the 19th century or as Japan has been in the 20th century? Anthropologists and historians of India have contributed much to the view that India is changing, but that the process of change and the content of what is changing will not necessarily follow the pattern of change we have become so familiar with in Western societies. To conclude an essay in which I have essentially taken a view that continuity and change have been constant in India, I would like to speculate about the future of its society and culture and, in particular, to put forth an argument about the possibility of radical and rapid social and cultural change. I will identify five components in the current situation in India as the dynamics of social change: the growth of population and the changing demographic composition of the Indian population, the social as well as the economic effects of greatly increased agricultural yields—the "Green Revolution," the increase of region-wide communication systems and the development of strong regional identities, the effects of the change in elite structure, and the consequences of modern mass democratic politics for the social structure.

In recent years, a great deal of attention has been paid to the effects of the growth of the Indian population on the Indian economy. It is estimated that the Indian population is now more than half a billion people. As fast as agricultural production seems to be increasing, the population is also increasing. In most demographic discussions the emphasis centers on questions of the need to limit the Indian population if the country is to develop its economy successfully. Apart from concern about its magnitude, a number of questions about the rising Indian population needs to be asked. The growth of the Indian population appears to be based on two processes: first, a lower rate of infant mortality so that more of the children born in recent years reach adulthood; and second, the fact that those who reach adulthood live longer. Forty-one percent of the Indian population in 1961 were under the age of 14, and 32 percent were between the ages of 15 and 34.[1]

More people are born and are living longer lives. What happens to deeply held cultural values about age when there are a lot of very young people around and also an increasing number of elderly people? Perhaps a society can sustain a veneration of the aged only when there aren't many aged around. Much time has been spent by social scientists in arguing about the past, present, and future of the Indian joint family. Oddly enough, little attention has been devoted to the ideology of the joint family and to the accepted pattern of authority within it, which grants the most authority to the oldest member. Perhaps the culture, rather than the form or structure of the joint family, will change as more and more men reach their forties and even their fifties before they can inherit land because their fathers are living longer. The culture of the joint family may have been maintained by a demographic artifact, that there weren't too many grandfathers around for too long, so that the possibility of a three-generation family living together was not all that frequent. Now, more and more women will be living past middle age, their children grown, and will still be in households under the domination of the mothers-in-law. The change in the age structure, with more young around and more elderly remaining in positions of authority, may lead to changes in the culture, and particularly that of the family.

The absolute growth in population will have consequences for the social structure as well. As was discussed above, the day-to-day functioning of the caste system depends on the knowledge that can only be gained in a face-to-face group. Caste, as an interaction system, and the maintenance of local caste hierarchies depends on knowing to what groups individuals belong and what behaviors are expected from them. Caste, as an aspect of the culture, is constantly reinforced by the pattern of interactions. In the urban setting, caste is less based on interactions across caste lines and more on an attributional system in which the gross characteristics of a person determine behavior, both of a caste

[1] Government of India, Ministry of Information and Broadcasting, *India: A Reference Annual 1969* (New Delhi 1969), p. 10.

and of a noncaste nature. As the population of India increases, the size of villages increases and the percentage of people living in large villages increases. In 1951, approximately 25 percent of the rural population lived in villages of more than 2,000 people; in 1961, the percentage rose to 31 percent.[2] If this trend has continued, as much as 40 percent of India's rural population may be living in large villages today. Can the face-to-face aspects of the caste system be as effectively maintained in villages where, more and more, not everyone knows who everyone else is nor does he know about everyone else? In the large villages, inter-caste relations may become increasingly economic relations and contractual rather than intertwined with social and ritual relations. Will the interactional pattern by which the local caste system is maintained be able to continue when villages become larger? In the past, when villages became too big, they frequently fissioned into two or more villages. With land being almost totally occupied and with no possibility of founding new villages, it is possible that a new kind of Indian village will develop, and whatever aspects of community in a social and cultural sense existed will disappear. The village will gradually become only a residence site rather than a sociological entity.

In the last few years, discussion of Indian agriculture has shifted from the question of stagnation and lack of growth to questions about overproduction. Even excluding the good rainfalls in 1968 and 1969 leading to bumper crops, it is clear that new varieties of rice and wheat, the expansion and better utilization of water resources, and the use of chemical fertilizers are leading to an agricultural revolution. However, the ability to use the new agricultural technology is not uniform. It has been most successful in the Punjab, parts of Western Uttar Pradesh, and parts of Andhra Pradesh and Tamilnad. Even within the regions in which it has been most successful, the bigger farmers have been most able to take advantage of the innovations. Hence, the rich seem to be getting richer and the poor are getting poorer.

The expansion in agricultural productivity and rural wealth, even though uneven across the social structure and regionally varied, has also had important consequences for the nonagricultural segment of the economy. New irrigation facilities, in the form of tube wells, and the expansion of canal irrigation, have been based on the availability of new pumping equipment, both diesel and electric. This, in turn, has meant that the need for the development of mechanics has increased. The road network in India has been expanded. The movement of agricultural products by truck has become very common again, increasing the

[2] *Census of India, 1961*, 1, India, II A (i), 222.

need for many new skills—truck drivers, mechanics, and other service workers. More and more agricultural products are being processed in the rural areas and in small towns. Storage facilities have to be built. New wealth has been translated into new consumption patterns, ranging from the building of brick and cement houses to electrically operated hand pumps for running water to transistor radios, and an enormous increase in bicycle ownership.

Very often, the service needs of the new technology are being handled at the village level. There has been a real growth in technical skills needed in the villages. No longer is the village blacksmith, who could make and repair ploughs and other agricultural implements with simple tools and technology, sufficient to maintain the needs of the new agriculture; blacksmiths and others have had to learn new skills. It is possible that Indian industrialization will be more closely tied to local areas and to the agricultural economy than has been the experience in the West. The manufacture of parts, the assembly of simple machinery, and the servicing of new equipment may become as much a part of the village economy as was simpler craft production in older times. This possibility might mean that industrial development will be more diffuse here than it has been elsewhere. Although large urban-based industrial complexes will grow, it might be that a semi-industrialized rural economy will emerge that will absorb the surplus labor, often thought to be the concomitant of agricultural change. Thus, the pattern of rural-urban relationships in India may be very different than what we have known in the West. India may have two kinds of urbanized cultures; an urban middle class cut off from much of the countryside, as was argued in the preceding chapter, and a semi-urbanized countryside.

Political scientists and others have long worried about the increase in regionalization in India. The English language is being replaced increasingly by regional languages for higher education. The elite civil service and the national politicians have long had a cosmopolitan outlook based on their acquaintance with English, travel abroad, and an all-India perspective. However, there are both political and economic barriers to inter-regional migration. State governments fight for a principle of the distribution of resources on a regional rather than on a centralized planning basis. Most people argue that what is good for a State is good for India. The States are now almost entirely based upon linguistic boundaries so that the borders of a State tend to be the borders of a regional language. A number of political movements, such as the D.M.K. in Tamilnad and the Shiv Sena in Maharashtra, have a regional and not an all-India appeal. There is much concern that in 1972, the year of the next general election, the Congress Party, which has been the national ruling party since 1946, will lose its majority and the national level will become so weak in the political system that India will be "Balkanized."

In emphasizing the negative aspects of the growth of regionalism, much that is positive and dynamic in the social and cultural system tends to be overlooked. While communication on an inter-regional basis may be declining, although this is not clear, intra-regional communication is increasing enormously. The number of students in schools at all levels has roughly tripled since 1950. It is estimated by the Indian Ministry of Information that there are 69 million students in schools in India, 25 million in secondary schools and two million in colleges and universities. In 1950 there were 400,000 college students.[3] The significance of these figures lies in the expansion of the knowledge of regional languages along with the learning of other skills. A generation is coming of age in India in which both speaking knowledge of and literacy in the regional language are going to be very widespread. The use of the standard regional languages and the possible decline of local and subregional vernaculars mean the possibility of much more effective communication. Not only do the primary and secondary schools further the establishment of the primacy of the regional standard languages but also, of the regional cultures as well. School children learn about the past of their States and their heroes. An identity as a Bengali or a Maharashtrian or a Tamilian is strengthened not only for the elite in these regions but also for the population at large.

This strengthening of regional identity may be at the expense of identity as an Indian. However, it must be remembered that people are now identifying with States that range upwards of 80 million people and with smaller states with populations of fifteen to twenty million. It is an open question whether the idea of nation state developed in Europe during the 19th century is functional for a society of the scale and vastness of India. It might be that the States, whether they be independent nations as we have known them for the last 100 years, or associated in a much looser federal union than is now characteristic of India, may be more viable than efforts to maintain a highly centralized nation state on the English or even the American model. The movement to stronger regional identity with more political control at the State level may lead to better governance.

The rise in education is thought by some to be accompanied by a decline in the quality of education, particularly at the higher secondary and the college and university level. India has been justifiably proud of the graduates of its major universities and elite colleges, such as Calcutta

[3] Government of India. Ministry of Information and Broadcasting, *India: A Reference Annual* (1969), p. 60.

University, Elphinstone College in Bombay, and St. Stephens in Delhi. Since the early 19th century, higher education in India has been premised on an elite model, with very small numbers being highly and effectively educated. The elite civil service and the liberal professions, including university teaching, have been based on this model. The national leadership has been drawn for the last twenty years from this highly educated English using elite. Political pressure led to a demand to alter this elite model in favor of a mass model. The newer generation of State and national politicians and, to some extent, of the State civil servants is now drawn from populations of different backgrounds and experiences. The smaller towns and the rural areas are tending to be better represented in the State civil service and in the State legislatures. It is not unusual to find political leaders who do not use English and to find civil servants who, although they may understand English, are not comfortable using it. Many more official transactions take place in the regional languages than was formerly the case. The spread of education is challenging an older elite whose position was based on its English education. The new elite's style and background may be closer to the mass of the population of its regions. Certainly communication will be easier because they share a common language and culture.

Finally, the major dynamic for social change appears to come through the political process. Electoral politics has meant competition and bargaining in order to be elected to office. The landless and the poor now have a second resource, in addition to their labor, that can be used in their relations with the landed, rich and powerful—their votes. Often votes are sought after through traditional lines of power. A landlord may try to bring pressure on his tenants to vote for him. But, as was discussed above, with competition for office or support within the landlord group, the tenants often find one or more persons from the landlord group seeking their votes. In this competition for votes, promises must be made and, even if they are not kept, lower status people in the society find they have something other people want. They are givers and not receivers and since status in Indian society is tied to the idea that it is the higher person who gives and the lower status person who receives, elections have the effect of challenging one of the basic cultural tenets of the society.

Politics has opened up another channel of mobility and influence in the society. A parallel hierarchy has been established that is based on different principles than that represented by the caste system and the long-standing administrative system. Numbers rather than status can be important in establishing power in a system with electoral politics. Even the Untouchables, as was seen in the discussion of the Jatavs of Agra, can make themselves felt through political organization in a way that is new in the society.

Since the 1920s, when the Congress Party reached down to try to mobilize rural strength for the nationalist struggle, new ideological messages have been circulating in the society. It is easy to dismiss much of the admonitions to equal treatment found in the Indian Constitution as hollow rhetoric but in a society in which the *Raj* has always set styles for the culture of the masses, the effects of an egalitarian ideology can be felt by the mass of the population.

The potential for radical change may exist in the present society even though it may take another generation to see these changes become widespread. With different elites less tied to the British ruling tradition, with demographic changes leading to changes in the rural social structure in village forms, with more rural wealth and a kind of urbanization of parts of the countryside, and with wider acceptance of egalitarian ideas growing from the political system, India could be radically transformed. If some of these speculations have any reality, what kind of society would result from these changes? It could be that caste would be reduced to a regulator of marriage and that many of its associated functions that have characterized it for the last two hundred years may be replaced. Economic groupings might become more important in the society. If there emerges a rich, modern, successful farming group, as distinct from the old landlord group, with landless workers who are viewed less as dependents in the traditional fashion and more as labor, and if there is an increasing number of skilled and semi-skilled service workers in the countryside, then a rich peasantry, a large landless field working population, and semi-skilled service workers might replace castes as the operative social categories in the rural areas.

The State could become much more important than either the local area or the nation in a cultural sense. People would identify with their regional culture, which could be more uniform than it has been in the past. The top status groups in the State would be drawn from different elites whose education and experience would be more closely tied to their regional cultures. Regional variants of Hinduism might replace the more generalized civilization-wide Hinduism that developed in the 19th century with reform movements such as the Arya Samaj and the Ramakrishna Mission.

As a political system, India might be much less centralized than it is today. The national civil service would be reduced in its significance. The major political arena would be the State capitals rather than New Delhi. Centralized planning would be extremely difficult.

Could basic institutions like the family change? As was noted above in the discussion of Westernization, thus far the educated middle class, which itself has been traditionally reared, has been successful in maintaining ties with its traditions because of the presence of the household as the major socializer of the next generation. As education increases amongst middle-class women, both in the cities and in the countryside, and as the ideology of the joint family comes into question through demographic change, it is possible that more and more educated women and their husbands would take on direct responsibility for socializing their children. Therefore, the new elites, steeped in a modern form of their regional culture, would raise their children differently than they themselves had been raised.

India, in the last decades of the 20th century, might be quite a different society than the one that we have known in the middle of the 20th century. It will not be like Western Europe or the United States in social structure, given the scale of the societies involved, the continuing large component that lives in its rural segment, and with the possibility of the emergence of a new kind of semi-rural urbanization pattern. There could be major changes in the culture, but this would seem less likely than changes in social structure, with the strengthening of the regional cultures, all of which are centered on the basic cultural premises that have characterized Indian civilization for the last millennium.